EXTRAORDINARY ORDINARY WOMEN

by
Alice Hellstrom Anderson

Ladybug Press
San Carlos, CA

Copyright © 1998 Alice Hellstrom Anderson
Cover and graphic design Copyright ©1998 Georgia Jones
First printing 1998
Printed in the United States of America

Library of Congress Cataloguing in Publication Data
Alice Hellstrom Anderson
        Extraordinary Ordinary Women: Making a Difference

Sociology

ISBN 1-889409-20-0 (pbk)

                                        97-76405

15% of net from this book is being donated to Guide Dog Foundation for the Blind, Inc.®

ON THE COVER:

TOP ROW, LEFT TO RIGHT:
        ANITA MARTINEZ, COLENE DANIEL, VIVIAN CASTLEBERRY
MIDDLE ROW, LEFT TO RIGHT:
        IVY GILBERT-VIGUE, NANCY SCHOCH, JA'NETTE AGOSTO
BOTTOM ROW, LEFT TO RIGHT:
        JANE MARSTON, REV. THALIA DRAKE JILLSON, MARGARET CHASE SMITH

About the Author

Alice Hellstrom Anderson lives on a quiet lake in Maine where she publishes a small local newspaper. Her positive attitude and optimistic outlook attract people with similar goals: to encourage and help others enjoy an abundantly blessed life, no matter the circumstances. She has been an educator, a missionary, a public speaker, an entrepreneur and a publisher. Her faith in God manifests itself in her zest for life and in her writing as she tells the stories of women who are role models for everyone, regardless of gender, age, or status in life. "It isn't so much what life hands you," she says. "It's what you do with it that determines the quality of your life. We can all learn how to live more successfully from the role models we meet every day -- ordinary extraordinary people who unconsciously teach us by example."

Although she has prepared half a dozen book manuscripts for other authors, and has written many articles and stories for her own publications, Extraordinary Ordinary Women is Anderson's first published book.

Preface

It's quiet on the cove in the early mornings. That is, the people who live here are quiet. If you know how and when to listen, however, you'll hear the other inhabitants conducting a quiet symphony of their own.

Outside my bedroom window, the sun rises first, lighting the stage with a soft peach glow. Cobweb kingdoms hastily built by busy spiders decorate the stage with deceptively fragile geometric designs. Sometimes the loons lift the first strains of the symphony with a soft tremolo, chatting to each other about the day's schedule, deciding which of them will take the kids for their swimming lessons. Sometimes the opening measures are the brass section of red squirrels chattering over the sunflower seeds, discussing the rise and fall of the stock market, no doubt. But most often it's the string section of birdsong that wakes me to a new day of opportunity. Myrtle warblers, gold and purple finches, and chickadees produce an original melody while others, less melodious (great blue herons, barn swallows, mallards and hooded mergansers) provide choreography with flits, swoops, whooshes, dips and hops.

Occasionally someone solos center stage. It might be the busy hummingbird with no time to stop for a drink, hovering frantically at the feeder. (I call him the piccolo.) Often it's the beaver who cavorts like an otter, lying on his back or doing a full roll just for the fun of it. Once it was a turkey vulture who just sat there in my neighbor's tree, resting his six-foot wingspan for a full twenty minutes! One glorious morning it was the Canada Geese, proudly introducing their newly hatched fluffy goslings. Whoever solos, it's bound to be a great performance.

Just under the mirror surface of the water, perch, bass, pickerel, and an occasional salmon or trout jockey with the turtles for the opportunity to hold a note or insert a rest, providing an opportunity to savor the symphony. Throughout the day, the woodpeckers provide a staccato rhythm that keeps the music moving steadily toward evening, when the loons call a wobbly goodnight as they swim from the cove to the larger lake beyond. They'll settle the kids in the nest for the night and be back in the morning. It's a lengthy composition, lasting the entire day, every day, from May to October. Can you tell that I love it?

For some of us, life is more a cacophony than a symphony. It is a constant struggle to make ends meet, find the right job, marry the right person, meet that deadline or just make it through one more day. Some sail through life's challenging moments with grace and glory, performing their own symphony that leaves us all better for having heard it. Others flounder and spiral downward and never seem to get back on track. Theirs is an unfinished symphony. What makes the difference?

There are certain inner qualities that determine how a person approaches life. These are gifts at birth, and we all receive some. What makes ordinary people extraordinary is how they handle the gifts they have been given.

In 1993 my partner, David, and I started publishing a small local magazine about women who demonstrated these inner qualities by reaching out to help others with no thought of reward. We honored one woman on the cover and we filled the magazine with informative articles written by professionals in their areas of expertise. We called it The Maine Woman. Every month for almost four years we introduced our readership to these role models. They weren't hard to find. They were everywhere -- ordinary, extraordinary women giving of themselves to help people cope with life's difficult situations.

By the time we reached 30 issues we were hearing from women all over the country, recommending women for the cover stories. We changed the name to *The New England Woman*. After 39 issues we stopped printing, changed the name to *The Women's Pages* and expanded globally by putting the entire magazine on the Internet.

Then I moved into a 70-year old cottage on a lake. And my life was immediately inundated with ladybugs. Every day for over four months I caught around 100 of the friendly little invaders. I have always considered ladybugs benign and helpful, but when they began falling off the ceiling into my morning coffee, it was time to get serious. I searched the Internet for help. (You can find *anything* on the Internet, I had been told.) I surfed for ladybugs and found *Ladybug Press* and Georgia Jones, the nicest publisher anyone could hope to meet! She was looking for writers. I queried; she responded. You're holding the result in your hand.

Many of the women you'll meet in these pages were honored on the covers of *The New England Woman* magazine. Others were referred by friends and acquaintances who knew I was working on a book. All are inspiring and have enriched my life. I trust reading their stories will enrich yours as well.

And lest I leave you hanging, the ladybugs have moved outdoors for the summer, where the symphony of the cove is in full voice.

Thanks to...

My friend for life and beyond, Jude Hannemann, who took a chance and agreed to be the very first cover woman on the magazine in 1993. Just look what she started!

All the women whose stories you hold in your hand. Without their gracious willingness to share their strengths and weaknesses with us, we would all be poorer. Special thanks to Susan Stanford-Rue, who graciously allowed me to quote heavily from her book *Will I Cry Tomorrow?* in the telling of her story.

The people who referred me to the women who were not alumnae of the magazine, proving once again that it's not **what** you know, it's who you know: Ja'nette Agosto, Nina Beaty, Wayve Berg Bradley, Vivian Castleberry, Lynn Crystal, Cyd Davidson, Derek de Cambra, Anna Gould, Ivy Gilbert-Vigue, Audrey Jones, Cheryl Jones, Jane Marston, Lucille Sollenberger **and** *Lois Toomer*.

My inner circle of friends: Ivy Gilbert-Vigue **and** Millie Cooper Hinken **who proofread endless copy and kept me on the straight and narrow, and** Jane Marston, **who consistently encouraged me with her enthusiasm and by buying me lunch. All who suffered may now rejoice!**

My mother, Blanche Hellstrom, who did not only her own household chores, but most of mine as well while I was chained to the computer.

My neighbors on the cove, Mildred and Lawrence Phillips, **who politely listened to me read my own book aloud!**

Erin Henry, the best student intern any author ever had!

And last, but maybe most noteworthy of all – *the ladybugs!*

Introduction

The women you are about to meet are ordinary, everyday women. Their ages range from 16 to 97. They represent different parts of the country, different occupations, and different approaches to life's problems. Yet they all share several qualities in common -- perseverance, self-esteem, wisdom, faith, creativity, and a sense of purpose and commitment. Collectively, and individually, their most stellar quality is the ability to give something back to life in order to help others.

Like most ordinary people in the course of daily life, each of these women saw a situation in the world that needed to change. What makes these ordinary women *extraordinary* is that they did something about it! What they did to effect change and how they did it is the stuff that usually doesn't make the front page of the newspaper. But it makes for heart-warming and life-challenging reading! They are role models for us all.

In telling their stories, I used mostly their own words, held together by a few observations of my own. What they told me, I share with you.

To David Anderson

my business partner
my encourager and supporter
my ex-husband,
my best friend.

Table of Contents

EXTRAORDINARY ORDINARY WOMEN

Claudette Thing

Volunteer Isn't Something She Does To Feel Good About Herself

Like most of us, Claudette Thing didn't like feeling helpless when dealing with life's challenges. Characteristically, she went out and did something about it. She determined what skills she needed and then set herself the task of finding out where she could acquire those skills. In the process, she helped improve the lives of others.

Claudette got her degree at the University of Maine, but she got her education elsewhere. Her life experiences have proven as valuable as her schooling, if not more so. "I needed to balance academic knowledge with practical experience, and to do this at my own pace," she explains. "For me, school was the last place I wanted to go for an education. After getting my degree, I worked for several years and then I decided to design the package of knowledge  I wanted. I started at the League of Women Voters. I spent seven years there in various capacities, all issues oriented. After I completed my term as president of that group, I was asked to be on the legislative committee for the United Way, where I served for twelve years, the last three as chairperson. That membership began my journey into social service volunteerism and expanded my view of the human condition. I joined the State Budget and Income Maintenance subcommittee. It was a solid education regarding the human care priorities of our state government and how citizens can participate in shaping those priorities. I soon realized that by influencing the public policy that deals with basic human needs, an individual could touch the lives of so many more people than is possible by dealing with one person, one problem at a time. Human care issues are so numerous and so complex that no legislator can possibly be an expert in all of them. Volunteers who work with one person, one problem at a time can help decision-makers sort out these issues by sharing the experience and perspective that they have developed through their volunteer work.

One volunteer commitment eventually expanded into another as Claudette searched for ways to improve her skills and her contribution. She volunteered to be an interviewer for United Way Volunteer Center, which collected requests for volunteers from approximately 160 nonprofit organizations, and helped match volunteers with over 600 agency requests. It also provided training for nonprofit agencies on volunteer management. "Gradually, I learned how services weave together to provide a fabric of care in the community. I felt I was helping to support the work of the nonprofit agencies by connecting them with valuable human resources."

When the Volunteer Lawyer's Project, which provides free legal services to low income residents, was looking for intake workers to assess people's eligibility for services, Claudette saw an opportunity to say thank you to the community for helping her develop her interviewing skills, as well as an opportunity to learn more about the legal system. "Although assessing client eligibility sounds simple and straightforward, it isn't," she says. "People calling for help are often dealing with fear, anxiety, frustration, confusion or anger. Intake workers have to deal with all those emotions to get at the information required. Most often the callers do not qualify for services. I did this work for those callers who did not meet the eligibility criteria. Those callers could feel totally alone when they heard that they would not get free legal services. By spending a few minutes to acknowledge their feelings and helping them to identify other resources for dealing with their situation, I could encourage them to go forward on their own. I could give them hope." It was that desire to give hope and encouragement to people who had to tackle their legal problems alone that led Claudette to further volunteer as a Family Law Advisor. "My job was to help people understand the mechanics of doing their own divorce, custody, visitation or child support amendments. Volunteers did not give legal advice. We helped calm fears by demystifying the legal process and reassuring people that they did, indeed have the ability to address their family law issues, if they just took it one step at a time. My greatest satisfaction came from the opportunity to give people the information to help themselves."

It was that interest in giving others knowledge to help themselves that led Claudette to the two most significant jobs of her volunteer career: Sexual Assault Survivor Advocate and Crisis Intervention Counselor. "These were the most urgent and worthwhile activities that I have ever undertaken. The training was rigorous, the volunteer schedule was demanding and the work was intense. I was never so energized and exhausted at the same time. These two jobs not only gave me a tremendous sense of being needed, they also gave me skills that I could use in my own life. Before I was given the expert crisis intervention training given by Ingraham, a local mental health agency, I didn't know how to respond to friends or family members who shared their pain with me. Ingraham taught me how to listen to people with empathy rather than pity, and how to help them turn emotional chaos into order. The approach to crisis intervention is very structured. The steps we are taught to follow help the caller to focus on a plan of attack rather than on the problem itself. You can't take away peoples' problems, but you can help them see where they have control over the situation. Ultimately, it is that sense of control, that awareness of a possible course of action that provides the most relief." One of the most memorable calls Claudette received on the hotline was from an elderly woman who was threatening suicide. Based on the protocol crisis workers are taught to apply in determining the severity of a suicide call, she knew this was the highest probability situation. The caller had no hope, had a clear plan and had the means to execute her plan. "I wanted to reach in through the phone to stop her, but my words were my only recourse. It was a long and draining call, but at the end of it the caller had decided to give life another chance. Before we said goodbye, the woman said to me, 'I don't know, but I kind of love you.' When I went to bed that night, I felt that I had truly earned my place on earth for that day. It was that kind of experience that made all the work worthwhile."

Lest anyone get the impression that the skills Claudette has developed through her volunteer work keep her in complete control of her own problems at all times, she is quick to add that she has her share of down times as well. "I know firsthand how important it is to have someone in your life who encourages you to keep going. I have an extraordinary friend who is a constant support. I have a perfectly wonderful husband who is truly the wind beneath my wings. And, I have ideal parents who have always given me a sense of security and stability."

In much of the work she has done, Claudette has seen children who haven't had the benefit of that security and stability. These children spend their childhoods trying to protect themselves or trying to meet their basic emotional or physical needs. Their suffering eventually affects all of society. She believes that by doing what we can to help children get the security and stability they need to thrive, we can make the world a better place for all of us. That belief lead her to serve on a citizen review panel for the substitute care program of the state Department of Human Services. "This position was my first personal contact with the issue of child abuse and neglect. Citizen panel members reviewed the case plans developed for children in state custody and participated in case review meetings. Each case was reviewed every six months to determine the status of the plan and the family's progress toward reunification. The role of the panel member was to bring a community perspective to these reviews and to increase the pool of ideas for helping the family to get back together. As part of this work, I learned about foster care, adoption, emergency shelters, group homes, child protective procedures, the operations of the state Department of Human Services, substance abuse, fetal alcohol syndrome, family violence, Medicaid reimbursements, learning disabilities, school policies, adolescent pregnancy, housing and much more. It seemed that all of our social concerns intersected in the issue of child abuse. I saw the weaknesses and the impact of our existing public policies on the lives of individuals. For example, the policy that promotes family reconciliation often results in the child having to wait for years before he or she arrives at a permanent living arrangement. It was heartbreaking to see children moving through a succession of foster homes, group homes, or even emergency shelters as they waited for family issues to be resolved. Meanwhile they became more depressed, anxious, or alienated and more distracted from their schoolwork. The experience increased my conviction that ordinary people, who have firsthand contact with peoples' struggles, have a vital role to play in influencing the public policy decisions made by our public officials. It also propelled me to find a way to help families sooner, before they break apart."

When a local program called Youth Alternatives, Inc. asked her to participate in their family mediation program, she saw the request as that early opportunity she was looking for to help families and children. It was also good opportunity to apply the experience she gained as a volunteer consumer mediator for the state attorney general's office, while at the same time expanding it into a new area of expertise. She has been a mediator with the program since 1990. "My greatest reward from this activity came from a case that presented no hope of a reconciliation between parents and child. Although the adolescent wanted to return home, the parents had suffered as much conflict as they felt they could bear without totally destroying the family. We were meeting to help them decide where else, other than the family home, the child could live. When a family member refused to sign the agreement they had reached by the end of our first session, I was loosing hope that any positive resolution to this conflict was possible. As we scheduled the second session of this mediation, I secretly wondered why I should give up my precious Saturday for what promised to be a futile exercise. But my co-mediator and I persisted. After many hours of taking one step forward and three steps backward, the family devised an agreement which allowed the child to return home. The family members left the mediation with smiles on their faces. They had renewed hope for the future and joy over having found a way to preserve their family relationship. It was five days before Christmas. When my co-mediator and I finished with this case, we felt that we had just experienced the true meaning of Christmas. Christmas that year was one of the sweetest I have ever known."

Claudette has used her accumulated knowledge to serve on several boards and committees. "I've done almost everything: public relations, finance, fundraising, marketing, nominating, executive committee, strategic planning, and volunteer development. "These tasks are the unglamorous work of organizations. Nobody gives you a hug, nobody

5

tells you that they '... kind of love you' when you do this work. Your satisfaction comes from knowing that you are helping to provide the supports which ultimately allow the services to reach those in need."

After spending over twelve years volunteering in all aspects of the human care system, Claudette started to wonder if she were overlooking an opportunity to have an even greater impact on the effort to reduce human suffering. It seemed to her that preventing people's problems would be much more humane than working to fix them after they have occurred. When the local United Way asked her to chair a committee to examine the nature of prevention and to recommend how prevention could be incorporated into the work, she eagerly said yes. Claudette became convinced that primary prevention (services and activities provided before harm ever occurs) needs more attention. "Society can ill afford the financial and emotional costs that come when we wait for problems to occur, or get serious before we do anything. For example, it is cheaper and more humane to install smoke detectors, teach people fire safety, and ensure building code enforcement than it is to find new housing for a family whose house has burned, or to provide extensive medical, psychological, and rehabilitative treatment for the victim of a fire. I'm not sure where my next volunteer job will be, but it will certainly be one that promotes primary prevention. Getting at the root causes of problems may not seem as urgent as dealing with immediate problems, but it is the approach I believe holds the most promise for reducing the need for help. I'd rather work to keep smiles on peoples' faces, rather than work to wipe away the tears."

Although Claudette's volunteer commitments have practically constituted a full time job, she doesn't see her contribution as especially generous. "I had the freedom to devote a lot of time to these activities. People who have full-time jobs, children, aging parents to care for and also volunteer are the generous ones. They get a lot of respect from me. My contribution is also not generous because I have gained much from my volunteer work. I became a volunteer to develop skills and gain knowledge, and I achieved both of those objectives. In the process I was rewarded because I felt needed and appreciated by those whose struggles I have shared. The most satisfying aspect of volunteer service for me has been the extent to which I was able to empower others. I don't like to think of volunteer work as going out to save people. I think that attitude only helps to keep people in the victim role. I don't want to save people. I want to help them help themselves. Encouraging that self-reliance ultimately reduces the need for services and makes for a happier, healthier society."

Claudette believes strongly in volunteerism. "Volunteering provides value all round. It helps others, it's good for the person volunteering, and it strengthens our communities. It builds what is called social capital, that is, the conditions that facilitate coordination and cooperation for mutual benefit. Everyone has a talent or an interest that can be shared with someone else. It doesn't matter whether you do a little or a lot, or whether you do administration or direct services. The important thing is to get involved."

Most of us volunteer with one organization and feel we've done our part to make the world a better place. We volunteer in order to help others, of course, but also to make ourselves feel good. What makes Claudette unusual is her attitude toward volunteerism. She puts the emphasis not on what she's done, but on what she has received in return. She's very candid about what all this altruism has done for her. "I don't want to be idealized. I didn't volunteer in order to save anyone," she explains. "I wanted skills and knowledge, and volunteering was a good way to get them. As a result, I was able to empower people to overcome difficulties in their lives, so I've been twice blessed by my volunteer work. That's all the reward I need." That's how this vivacious, attractive young woman sees life: one huge opportunity. There are hundreds of people who are grateful she sees it that way.

Donna Short and
Meredith Bruskin

Camping for Families Affected by HIV/AIDS

The Human Immunodeficiency Virus (HIV) hurtles over any boundary, affecting people from all walks of life. It is not a disease confined to one group of people. Anyone can get it, and in a variety of ways. In 1990, two women, Donna Short and Meredith Bruskin, recognized that no one was providing any kind of emotional support for the children affected by HIV/AIDS, whether they had the virus or disease themselves, or if one of their parents or a sibling had it.

The needs of these children were being ignored, and that was unacceptable to Donna and Merrie. They decided to do something about it.

Donna Short runs her own construction company, and Meredith Bruskin has been a nurse for eighteen years, ten of them in the emergency room. By 1990, both of them had lost several very close friends to HIV/AIDS and were aware of the stigma on not only those infected, but those affected by it. They were both working as volunteers with the Waldo/Knox AIDS Coalition, and were part of a support group for people affected by HIV/AIDS. They had attended many a memorial service and were both looking for something positive to do that would make a difference.

9

In talking with the Department of Human Services, they discovered that the state had no program for helping children or families dealing with the challenge of HIV/AIDS, and that they had been receiving requests for respite care. Families needed a break from dealing with the disease – a place to just relax and not worry what people would think if they divulged that someone in the family was HIV positive.

"A small support group of eight of us thought we'd offer a week of respite for children," Donna remembers. "When we contacted people, they were hesitant to send the children on their own, because they hadn't yet opened up and told people they were dealing with this. So we had to invite the parents. We thought they could take day trips to shop and leave the children with us at the camp for activities. That seemed to relieve their minds and the first session of Camp Chrysalis was held in the summer of 1990 at a large inn. Twelve children, eleven moms and one dad attended. It was much more than we had expected. That first year, the connection was so strong, the staff decided a year was much too long to wait to connect with each other. A winter reunion was planned at another inn. It, too, was a wonderful success. The third session was held at a rented campground."

"We discovered that the parents had had no opportunity to network with other families dealing with HIV or AIDS," Merrie adds. "This was in the early days of public awareness, when people still thought you could catch AIDS by casual contact. We were just beginning to discover how the HIV virus spread, and how it did not. Part of the problem was that people were afraid to talk about it, and that fear only exacerbated the problem."

"The parents who had accompanied those first twelve campers weren't interested in shopping; they never left the camp! Instead, they were up until two every morning, talking about what it meant to live with HIV/AIDS. It became very apparent that they needed camp as much as the kids," Donna says. "It was total respite for them. They participated in the crafts and thoroughly enjoyed all the fun activities, as well as the serious, healing times of discussion and educational workshops. At that time, there were only three camps like this in the country. Ours was nonprofessional, volunteer, and all of the staff was affected (or infected) by HIV/AIDS. The idea was circular healing: for the staff to be doing this work was healing for us. And it was very healing for those who were HIV positive. We came to understand that the children always remembered to play every day. They really knew what living with HIV was about, and we learned from them. We simply provided the opportunity and the safe place. The word chrysalis is the safe cocoon where the butterfly develops its wings. It seemed a perfect name for our camp."

The camp session always starts with an opening circle where everyone has the opportunity to say something. When it was his turn, one unforgettable little boy burst out with, "AIDS, AIDS, AIDS, AIDS! I haven't been able to say that since camp last summer!" There are both emotional and spiritual elements of the camp, as well as workshops on different aspects of healing. Alternative methods of healing, legal issues, available resources, nutritional education and massage therapy – all have a place at Camp Chrysalis. People from the local community also donate their time as providers of special entertainment or workshops. Like the campers, some of the staff are HIV positive; some are not. Everyone works hard at presenting a balanced program and meeting the many needs on every level and of every age group. Participants (campers and staff) range in age from 3 to 70. A physician is on call and a registered nurse provides 24-hour coverage while camp is in session. Emergency facilities are nearby.

"We try to cover all the bases," Donna explains, "but this is a camp, so mostly we play! We don't sit around and talk about AIDS for a week. We have a good time. Swimming, boating, crafts, campfires are all part of the program, just as they are in any camp. We allow the children to come to knowledge about HIV/AIDS in their own way. Some don't mention it all week, even though they're surrounded by it. We accept HIV/AIDS as a fact of our lives. It helps the children gain a normalcy and a knowledge that neither they nor their parents are alone."

Camp Chrysalis is both confidential and free to all families. Donna and Meredith are co-directors and there is a working board of directors. The project is partially funded by private donations and partially by the Department of Human Services. Space is rented from a facility on a beautiful lake in Mid-coast Maine. All workers are volunteers who, like Donna and Meredith, use their vacation time to run the camp. The rest of the year is spent in fundraising.

What Camp Chrysalis is all about is the overwhelming power of connection and the realization that you aren't the only one in the world dealing with this. Two of the original campers were young boys who didn't know any other children were infected. The terrible loneliness gave way to immeasurable relief and instant friendship when they discovered each other. These are incredibly special bonds that are formed during Camp Chrysalis. All who attend have weathered loss of loved ones, bad times, hospitalizations, depression and fear. The bonding and healing are amazing to watch.

No one is more amazed than Donna and Meredith. "This idea became more than we could have ever hoped for," Donna smiles. "Attending the camp gives a person a much clearer view of what is going on. Petty things are set aside. Prejudices are broken down. Healing happens. It's wonderful to experience total acceptance. That's what we have all become to each other: a microcosm family of unconditional love."

Merrie adds, "That first week was very powerful, far beyond our expectations. We realized how many children were affected by having a family member infected, even if they were not. It was a terrifying time for people because of ignorance and fear. After the first week, when we could catch our breath, we realized this camp experience had to continue. We now have long-term survivors. We believe that is due in part to their willingness to face the truth. All the long-term survivors we know have come to grips with the fact that they are dealing with a virus, and they are dealing with it. The things that seem to help the most are a positive attitude, a change to a healthier lifestyle, and the truth."

"Right now," Donna explains, "our biggest problem is the camp's success! The 1997 session had 40 children and 15 adults. We're getting too big to maintain the intimate atmosphere which encourages the healing that comes from the freedom to be open. We don't want to lose that. This is the most powerful thing I've ever been a part of. It's not only allowed me to deal with the many levels of my own grief at losing loved ones to HIV/AIDS, but it has also taught me that the sum is much greater than all its parts. We need to open up our hearts and have tolerance for others. Camp Chrysalis is the ultimate tolerance. I believe there is great hope."

"I've been deeply involved with the healing arts all my working life," Meredith says. "but this is the most satisfying work I've ever done. During Camp Chrysalis, I see people deal with issues of class, race, sexism, homophobia and AIDS phobia. We start with a multiracial, multicultural group and we watch a community being forged. The issues around living with HIV take precedence and all the other prejudices just seem to melt away. That gives me hope that the world can change, and that we can live in peace and harmony. I only wish we didn't have to face a life-threatening disease to bring us together."

Ivy Gilbert Vigue

Investing Her Life to Help Women Achieve Financial Independence

Money occupies her mind, but it doesn't rule her life. Ivy Gilbert Vigue believes in living a *blended* — not balanced — life where there is no distinct separation between work life and home life. "It's unrealistic to expect a mother and wife to forget her family when she is on the job, and it's unrealistic to expect a businesswoman to forget her work the minute she gets home at night," says Ivy. "I accept the fact that my personal life will affect my professional life, and vice versa. That frees me to enjoy both."

Ivy has many different roles in her business life. She is the owner and C.E.O. of three companies: Firstmark Capital Corp., an investment advisory firm; FIRM Investment Corp., a broker-dealer; and Women & Investing, an advisory firm for women. She serves on the Board of Directors of Firstmark Corp., a multimillion dollar public company of which she was Chief Financial Officer for over twelve years. She is also C.E.O. of the Hamilton Foundation, a nonprofit organization that assists other charitable organizations in the endowment building process — a very busy and responsible position for which she volunteers her time. Ivy and her husband, Jim Vigue, founded the Hamilton Foundation for the purpose of giving something back to the community.

Ivy was raised by parents who believed you could do whatever you wanted to do in life, and encouraged their children to live up to their potential. Following her father's example, Ivy gravitated to figures and finances, choosing a career in financial planning and investments. Not long into her career, Ivy realized there was a real pattern forming. She found herself assisting more and more widows, divorcees and professional women in a position of less than adequate income and resources to maintain a sufficient lifestyle. It became obvious to her that there was a real need to educate women on the many financial issues that are so important today. She accepted the challenge head-on. Since that time she has specialized in assisting women in their pursuit of financial independence. Her seminars (which are free) are designed to assist women with their financial needs and introduce them to all areas of investing. "Women employ a different thought process than men do," Ivy explains. "When a woman explains financial principles to a woman, there's better comprehension, allowing women to begin taking control of their financial situations in a positive and confident manner. 80% of women are in financial jeopardy due to divorce or widowhood. That's two out of three. Without realizing it, women set themselves up for financial problems. Clearly there is a need for education in financial matters.

"I've watched a lot of financial advisors conduct client meetings in the last 15 years, and most of the time I got the impression the female client left the meeting not really understanding what the advisor had said. She often felt no control over her own financial future, having to put all her faith and trust in someone else, instead of herself. Women tended to rely on the men in their lives for financial advice, only seeking professional financial advice when they were either widowed or divorced. Usually a woman in this situation is dealing with a great deal of emotional stress and is not in the best frame of mind to understand what she needs to know in planning for her financial future. Common mistakes women make include putting all their assets in the market and not coming up with a diversified plan, investing in products of lesser quality, and agreeing to something they didn't fully understand. A woman's portfolio can include stocks and bonds, a retirement plan, cash — all of her assets over which she has control. The trick is to diversify, so all her assets aren't in the same basket. And it can be very confusing, especially if a woman allowed her husband to handle all the finances and suddenly she has to make the decisions.

"Women have been mentally conditioned to let their men handle finances. Think back to the 18th century. What happened to a woman's wealth? She wasn't entitled to it; it was considered her dowry and it was given to her husband. She had no rights to any of her money. Yes, we've come a long way, but you don't have to go back any farther than the last generation to see that things haven't changed that much. Many of us had mothers who kept their money in a shoebox on the closet shelf, or in a tin can at the top of the cupboard, or even stuffed under (or in) the mattress. That little cache of money they had scrimped to pull together was their security blanket.

"Little girls today need to be taught how to manage money. They need to know how to take control of their own financial well-being. We have to stop perpetuating the myth that someone else is going to take care of us financially. Case in point: if a woman allows her husband to handle the finances all their married life, and then they divorce after 20 or 25 years, she has to either hope the finances will be handled fairly or pay someone to make sure they are."

Where a woman seeks help at that juncture of her life is crucial to her financial future. If she seeks advice from an insurance person, she's going to end up buying insurance. If she seeks advice from a stockbroker, she's going to end up with stocks in her portfolio. So to whom should she turn? Ivy recommends that first of all, the person she turns to should be licensed in every area of investments — securities, insurance, all types of investments. Second, she should seek advice from a firm that is established and has a team in place. A one-man shop or part-time planner simply cannot keep up with all the changes in investments and regulations. Third, she should seek a firm with a good reputation. "Don't be afraid to call several successful businesswomen and ask them to recommend someone," she adds. "When you get the same name three times, you're probably on the right track.

"Everyone's situation is unique. A financial planner needs to see the entire picture — your goals, your projected needs, your lifestyle — in order to help you plan properly so you'll have the money you need when you need it or want it. Suppose you ask someone where you should invest $10,000. If they tell you to invest a particular way without asking your age,

17

your goals, your needs — without getting the whole picture, then you're not getting good advice and you should talk to someone else. It's impossible to give sound financial planning advice without knowing the whole scenario. The first step to financial security is building a firm foundation. That means protecting yourself from all possible loss with car insurance, life insurance, homeowner's insurance, retirement planning and emergency funds."

It's been gratifying to her to see the positive changes in the lives of some of the women she's consulted with. "The first year a woman is widowed or divorced is the hardest, of course. They're not only grieving and adjusting to life alone, but they have to make decisions that have far-reaching consequences when they're not in the proper frame of mind to do so.

"I've seen women in that position take courses and read books and consult with professional financial planners in order to make informed joint decisions about their finances and their future. They become active participants in their future and it does wonders for their self-esteem and sense of well-being. Some women become independent for the first time in their lives. And they love it! But first, they have to believe that they're worth it. It's hard to place value on running a household. Women have to learn to pay themselves first; take 10% right off the top and say this is for me. Set money aside for yourself.

"I never thought of myself as an educator," Ivy says with a smile, "but that's what I really am. I hate seeing people being taken advantage of. That's one of the reasons I absolutely love what I do. I get a lot of personal satisfaction when I can prevent even one woman from being taken in by poor advice, and I can see her make wise decisions and grow. Seeing a woman grow in her vision of herself and what she is capable of is a real high for me. I really love it when a woman client walks out of a meeting with me and feels that she understood what she needed to do financially for herself. I feel the same way about the women who work for me. I'm happy to spend time with them so they will also grow and move forward. It's very important to me. When I decided on financial planning for my career, there was no woman mentor for me to help me move forward or to pattern my career after. It was really hard to build credibility, no matter how many licenses I had. One of the ways I built credibility was to pursue and obtain the particular licenses in our field that require other licensees to report to me, called principal licenses. These licenses made me responsible for everything the people under me said, so everything had to go through me. That strategy began to build my credibility. I had to figure this strategy out for myself. I want to give my women employees the mentor I never had."

Ivy's commitment to educating women in financial matters prompted her to start a new company six years ago. She felt that a service and a newsletter with the title Women & Investing would be less intimidating for women. She was right. Her newsletter covers timely financial issues in a basic format that is both interesting and easy to understand. It is free for the asking. The first issue was mailed to 200 women. Now it goes to over 2,000 women all over the country.

Since both Ivy and Jim grew up in Maine, this is where they want to be and where they chose to raise their family. In the Gilbert-Vigue household, fiscal responsibility starts young. They have a fourteen-year-old son and a nine-year old daughter who both spend time at the office in order to understand their parents' business life. The fourteen-year-old follows his stocks and tracks his mutual funds, but he's no Alex P. Keaton. Both Ivy and Jim feel it's important for the kids to be well-rounded, so they are involved in all the academic and athletic activities as well as learning about finances. At this point, their son wants to be a major league baseball player and the nine-year-old wants to work in a toy store when she grows up! "Maybe she'll end up owning it," Ivy laughs. "We set no limits!"

Always looking for ways to help women take control of their finances, Ivy wants to get the message out to as many women as possible. In 1997 she published her first book, Women's Financial Wisdom: How to Become A Woman of Wealth. "I do a lot of public speaking, especially to women's groups," she adds. "The one message I'd like to get across to women is to take action. I think women wait too long to take control of their finances. It's never too late to start, but young women especially need to start setting money aside and investing for their future. Women need to educate their children and grandchildren. Age ten is not too young to have a mutual fund. For an investment of $25 a month, kids can learn a lot by watching the fluctuations. If you give your children an allowance, teach them to take 10% off the top and put it into savings. Another 10% can go to charity. It's important to have fun money, too. But it's also a lot of fun to watch a savings account grow!

"It's not good to have money be a constant worry. Then you're always struggling with the pennies and you'll never start saving the dollars. Like Murphy's Law, expenses do tend to eat up available cash. As your income increases, your expenses will, too. So unless you take that savings right off the top of your income, you'll never have the money to save. It's good to focus on income rather than expenses. Once you stop worrying about money you can start thinking of creative ways to move forward, such as getting more education or skills so you're eligible for a promotion. It's hard to break out of that mentality if you've been conditioned to just think about where the next loaf of bread is going to come from. You are responsible for your own financial situation. And your financial future depends on you. My goal is to break through all the mental conditioning women have experienced and to let them know they can take control of their finances and they can have a promising financial future.

"I believe life really is like the game of Monopoly. We all go around the board, landing on chance, paying rent, having things happen to us. And every time we pass go, we collect $200. That's our paycheck. But if we spend our entire lives just collecting $200 every time we go around the board, we'll never get ahead. That money is going to run out, unless we invest it. If we don't invest a portion, we can't win the game."

Here's one woman who has her priorities straight. She's a savvy businesswoman, a much-loved mother and wife, an esteemed leader for her employees, and a positive role model for all of us. Really successful people always seem to make time to help others, and Ivy is no exception. She is generous with her time, her wisdom and herself.

Ann Fassett

Providing Therapy on Horseback for People with Disabilities

Ann Fassett has loved horses since the day her grandfather sat her on the broad back of one of his work horses. "I had always wanted to ride," Ann remembers, "but my family could never afford a horse." After Ann married her high school sweetheart and had four daughters, they bought a horse. When the youngest daughter left for college, there was Ann with an empty nest and a beautiful Tennessee Walking Horse. "I was at loose ends, and it was a perfect opportunity to do something different," she explains. "For a long time I had had a dream of owning a farm of our own. Joe thought it was a good investment, and would save us the boarding bills for the horse, so we bought Briarhedge Farm in 1978, and I settled down to learn about riding."

Soon people began calling with requests for her to board horses. Never one to back down from a challenge, Ann built a 10-stall stable on the back side of the barn. "Neither Joe nor I knew one thing about running a stable, but Joe knew that with an empty nest on my hands, I needed another interest, so he was very supportive of the idea of starting a boarding business. I have a pet theory," she smiles. "I think that women who have been happy as mothers often turn to working with animals when the children go off on their own. It's the nurturing and the returned love from the animals that satisfies that mothering instinct."

Ann sought and received much help from the Equine Science Department at Ohio State University and the Soil Conservation Society, among others, in setting up the boarding stable. Soon the stable was full, and business was thriving. But she had a feeling there was more she could be doing. She was right. There was much more!

She had been reading about therapeutic riding in some of her horse magazines and journals and since she had been a volunteer for two years in the cerebral palsy clinic of the local hospital, it seemed natural to put the two together. After some research, she learned that many years ago, some German doctors had discovered that just sitting on a moving horse moved the human pelvis as if the person were walking. They had placed patients with disabilities or atrophied muscles on horseback and the results had been very encouraging. After World War II the British began using therapeutic riding on returning veterans. It had been very successful. "I kept thinking of the little kids in the cerebral palsy clinic with their deteriorating abilities and atrophied muscles," Ann remembers, "and I thought, What a great way to share this 50-acre farm!" It didn't take her long to put her resources and the needs of the kids together. Joe was all for the idea and told Ann, "Go learn all you can about starting a therapeutic riding program."

The first thing Ann did was attend a weekend seminar hosted by NARHA (the North American Riding for the Handicapped Association). In order to have a program that would operate most months of the year in Ohio, Ann needed an indoor arena. When it was completed in 1982, she approached her friend, Beverly Thompson, to help set up the nonprofit organization, the Equestrian Therapy Program, so they could accept donations and offer scholarships to those who could not afford the therapy otherwise.

"I had the farm, the stable, the indoor arena, the liability insurance (through NARHA), an idea and our nonprofit status. That was all we had," says Ann. "We needed horses, bridles, saddles, and volunteers – all requiring funds we didn't have. I approached the Lima (Ohio) Rotary Club with our needs, and they gave us a generous check for $2,000. Among other necessary items, we bought two Shetland ponies, a bridle and a saddle for $250. With a lot of help from NARHA and those two little ponies, Marybelle and Trigger, we launched our pilot program in the fall of 1983. We talked to the two local hospitals and chose eight students from the Developmental Therapy Program at St. Rita's Hospital and eight from the Cerebral Palsy Clinic at Lima Memorial Hospital. There was only one vital element missing: volunteers. We needed three volunteers for each student: one to lead the horse, and one to walk on either side. We talked to everyone we knew, and they showed up! It was a wonderful response. Those first sixteen kids did so well! We were thrilled with what we saw happening.

"In the pilot program, there was a little boy named Jim. He had a very short attention span and our instructor, Bev, had to keep reminding him to look at her. After three months, he was able to follow three consecutive commands. That was a huge achievement. I believe that children naturally want to do things when they're on horseback, probably because it's different than just being in a therapy room. They may be the same commands, but being on a horse makes them fun! I remember one little boy who had been totally nonverbal. As he came around the arena on Marybelle, he yelled, "Mom!" It was the first time he had spoken so that she recognized the word. Gradually, with continued speech therapy and therapeutic riding, he began to be more verbal. We believe the relationship with the pony unlocked his speech. Results like these are typical, and keep us all charged up!"

In 1984, the Equestrian Therapy Program began accepting adults. It was so successful that now 30 out of the 105 students are adults. Sixty percent of the students are children, some of them from four area schools which send multi-handicapped classes once a week. This program is very good for people with spinal cord injuries, head traumas, cerebral palsy, spina bifida or MS. If the muscles aren't totally gone, the motion of riding can encourage some tone into them. The first adult student in the program was a woman with MS, teaching in a middle school full time from her electric wheelchair. Because of her determination and her very strong faith, and because of the therapeutic riding program, she progressed from her wheelchair to two crutches, then to one crutch, and then to a cane. Today she runs beside a trotting horse and teaches all the adult classes. And she doesn't let them get away with a thing!

All adult students are asked the same question, "What do you expect to get from this program?" One woman in her early 70s with debilitating

23

Multiple Sclerosis answered, "If I could just drag my left leg into bed with me at night so my husband doesn't have to place it in the bed, I'd be happy!" She was never afraid of being on the horse, even though she had never been on one before. After the sixth week of therapeutic riding, as her husband wheeled her in, she announced with a big grin, "Last night I was able to drag my left leg into bed with me, all by myself!" Then she added, "I'm so tired of talking to people's belt buckles! My neck gets tired looking up at them from this wheelchair all the time. The greatest part of this program is sitting on that horse and looking down on people!"

There are as many different kinds of therapeutic riding centers in this country as there are needs. Some are a program just for the blind; some are just for patients in a particular rehabilitation hospital. Some of them operate only in the summer, using horses of 4H kids. Some centers are started by physical therapists, and that's all they do. Altogether there are 512 NARHA therapeutic riding centers across the U.S. of which 300 are accredited. Together, they helped 32,358 riders in 1996.

There are many ways of conducting a therapeutic riding program. Some programs have a full-time physical therapist on duty. The Fassetts and Bev hope to add that advantage to their program. After fifteen years, the program is still growing. As the financial manager, Joe is very much involved in the business, although not on a daily basis. There are over 70 men, women and teenagers who volunteer in the program, some of them have been there from the very beginning.

No one is turned away from the Equestrian Therapy Program if they cannot pay. The charge is $5 per session, and if that is not economically possible, a scholarship is given. The program doesn't receive any government grants, nor any contributions from the United Way. The $70,000 budget is met with donations alone. Ann and Joe do not receive salaries. The instructors receive an hourly wage per teaching hour and the staff is paid for taking care of the horses.

"We've grown slowly and steadily. We now serve a 10-county area," Ann adds. "We have always insisted on guaranteeing the quality of the work we do with the students, so we make sure every part of the existing program is working properly before we add anything new. One of the problems we encountered is how to get the students onto the horses – something you don't think about until you go to do it. Our instructors were having a lot of back problems due to lifting the disabled students from a mounting block. So, with the help of a local company, we invested in a hydraulic lift. It can go to any height and gently sets the rider on the horse's back, no matter how heavy the rider or how tall the horse. We also have a trapeze overhead which was donated by one of the hospitals. If adult students have the arm strength, they can use the trapeze to help get themselves onto the horses. That does a lot for their self-esteem. We have added staff as the program has grown. We now have three certified instructors and have apprenticed two more who will be going to a new therapeutic riding center north of here."

The program has three sessions per year, with the first class being a tour of the stables and an introduction to the horses. All the horses are donated, or are purchased with donations. Each animal must be healthy and have a good disposition — no nippers allowed! The horses used in the program really seem to enjoy it all. Chosen for their dispositions, they are given a long trial period. The staff put them through a lot of specialized training before a handicapped person ever gets on them. The horses sense that these are disabled riders and they are very gentle with them.

"The only reason this works is because of our horses," Ann explains. "I've seen even the nonprogram horses put their heads in the laps of the kids in wheelchairs when they're introduced. That kind of interaction usually dispels any fears the kids might have. The animals are wonderfully intuitive and seem to know that the children need to feel comfortable right from the very beginning."

Ann Fassett's vision and dedication to using her resources to help people through therapeutic riding have endeared her to all who work with her and know of her selflessness. She acknowledges the accolades with her own gratitude – to God (Whom she says worked hard behind the scenes!) and to the friends and volunteers who have contributed so much to help her to bring the dream to reality. "You never come out even," Ann says, as she encourages yet another disabled child to give a little more effort. "You always get back more than you put in!"

Ann has had the satisfaction of seeing her dream grow, and of course, the pleasure of seeing people improve physically and emotionally. "If you have the germ of an idea and you really want to see it happen, you can infect others with your enthusiasm and together you *can* make it happen. You have to have faith in God, in yourself, and in other people. Find something you want to do and just go for it! Nothing is really impossible!"

I Saw A Child

I saw a child who couldn't walk,
sit on a horse, laugh and talk.
Then ride it through a field of daisies
and yet he could not walk unaided.

I saw a child, no legs below,
sit on a horse and make it go
through woods of green
and places he had never been
to sit and stare,
except from a chair.

I saw a child who could only crawl
mount a horse and sit up tall.
Put it through degrees of paces
and laugh at the wonder on our faces.
I saw a child born into strife,
Take up and hold the reins of life
and that same child, I heard him say,
Thank God for showing me the way.

©John Anthony Davies. Used by permission.

Gloria Dugan

What She Does for Love

Gloria Dugan has a secret. And last year alone she shared it with over 26,000 people. The funny thing is, almost none of them even know her name. Gloria Dugan is the Executive Director of Catholic Charities Maine, the largest private, state-wide social service agency in the state.

With just over 700 employees and over 500 volunteers working within the 40 programs, projects and services of CCM at 24 different locations from one end of the state to the other, Gloria's days are full, challenging and rewarding. But personal satisfaction is not what motivates her. Want to know what it is? Love. The best kind of love: sharing the love God has shown her by spreading it around to those in need. Yes, she's been given a lot of responsibility. Yes, it consumes a lot of her time and energy. But Gloria would be the first to say she gets back more than she gives.

For a long time, Vermont was enough for Gloria. She grew up in a very small town nestled in the Vermont countryside. Gloria remembers, "My parents taught us that it was how we lived our lives that was important, and what we gave to other people was of lasting value." Neither of her parents were formally educated beyond the 8th grade, but they were extremely wise in the rearing of their two daughters, giving them guidance without being domineering, reasoning with them and considering the consequences of various courses of action, and then letting them make up their own minds. "I was always encouraged to think things through and then act accordingly," Gloria remembers. "I think there was a lot of praying and keeping the fingers crossed!" It worked. Gloria is the only member of her family who went on to complete college and then graduate school.

Although Gloria never had children of her own, her first love has always been working with kids. Her first job after college was in social work as a case aide at the Worcester Children's Friend Society, a foster care and adoption agency. Spotting her natural abilities, two women in particular, Marijane Jones, Gloria's supervisor, and the agency's director, Jean Griesheimer, mentored her, giving her more and more responsibility and just the right amount of prodding to keep her moving in the right direction. They suggested she get her master's degree, and offered her a scholarship to cover the cost. Believe it or not, Gloria refused! "I thought one degree was enough and set my sights right where they were. No farther!" Wisely, her mentors allowed her more responsibility within the foster care program. They assigned her to do some counseling with the unwed mothers who had given their babies up for adoption. After six months of silent strategy nudging her in the right direction, Gloria capitulated all on her own and decided that she could indeed do the job of a caseworker. So she agreed to get the required master's degree. Upon graduation, she became a caseworker in the foster care and adoption program where she stayed for three more years for a total of seven years. It was a happy and productive time for Gloria. She says, "If you believe in the dignity of the human person, and you can make a difference in just one life, that's what social work is all about."

Realizing that if she were going to grow professionally, she needed to make a move, Gloria set her sights on Vermont – where else? — to be a social worker with the state. They offered her a supervisory position, but, true to her convictions, she insisted on starting where everyone else started and working her way to supervisor. As she said then, "How can I supervise anyone if I don't know what they're dealing with?" It's a principle she still firmly believes. "I like supervision," Gloria admits with a smile. "I like helping people help other people."

In 1971 Gloria realized it was time for the next stage of her career.

She had been thinking of moving to Maine, so she called an old friend who just happened to work for Catholic Charities. She's been with them ever since.

Catholic Charities Maine is mission-driven. That means they find ways to do what they believe they were called to do: implement the social teachings of Jesus Christ as taught by the Catholic Church. From Aroostook to York, there isn't a county in Maine that doesn't benefit from this network of service delivery. CCM is staffed by, and serves, people regardless of race, religion, ethnic origin, gender, age or ability to pay.

Throughout the state, each social service program of CCM is headed by a fully trained professional staff member, supported by an effective and caring staff. Each program director works closely with related human service organizations, representatives of local, county, state and federal government agencies, community leaders, and a host of volunteers. While each program is uniquely directed to a specific population in need of service, close ongoing collaboration with others on the staff has been key to the agency's success. The commitment is to provide needed services regardless of ability to pay. However, in many instances, services are covered by third party insurance, Medicaid, and General Assistance. When possible, individuals pay privately, based on income guidelines. Funding is also received from a variety of sources, including the Roman Catholic diocese of Portland (covers all of Maine), all levels of government, local United Ways, and through the generosity of concerned businesses, foundations and individuals. In spite of its name, Catholic Charities Maine receives less than 5% of its 15-million-dollar budget form the Catholic Diocese. 84% of total revenue comes from reimbursement for services by the government; the remainder is a combination of gifts and donations, clients' contribution and third-party reimbursements.

After holding seven positions in the agency (including several newly created ones), Gloria was asked to be the Executive Director of Catholic Charities Maine - -the first woman (and the first non-Catholic) to hold that position. Her first responsibility was to take the agency through a reorganization. It was not an easy first assignment, but Bishop Gerry pledged his support and has been faithful to that commitment. Gloria's common sense approach to administration creates goodwill among those under her supervision and allows her coworkers to grow to their full potential. "I try to be fair, to be open, and to really listen to the people I work with," she says. "What we do here is help people to help themselves. We have a real team approach. I try to give my coworkers what they need to do the best job they can do. People of all different faiths work at CCM. The focus for employment is that the best person for the job fills the job. I have a super staff, and they're really very talented. That's how we get so much done!"

As a young woman, Gloria's natural tendency was to be satisfied with what she had, instead of entertaining grandiose ideas for her future. At every juncture of her career path, it was others who encouraged her to live up to her potential and take the next step. They knew what she didn't recognize in herself: a born leader, with a tremendous gift for administration. She uses that ability to guide those in her sphere of influence as they reach out to tens of thousands of men, women and children in need of encouragement, support and physical necessities. What makes Gloria so special? Her commitment to excellence, her compassion for others, her ability to bring out the best in her colleagues, and her personal integrity. Joseph J. Gerry, O.S.B., Bishop of Portland, put it this way: Ever mindful of the dignity of the human person, she now responds with vision to the social challenges facing our society as we enter the third millennium.

For over 27 years, Gloria Dugan has capably guided CCM with compassion and wisdom. She is an example of women in management at their best – coaxing the best out of people, and boosting their self-esteem in the process. She's rewarded with a sense of accomplishment, high employee morale and loyalty, and the happiness that comes from knowing you've helped someone. It's a winning combination that works for everyone involved.

Lillian Files

Bringing Back the Bluebirds

If you look quickly, you might see a petite blonde woman scurrying around the edges of a golf course, a wooden box under her arm. She's not carrying golf clubs. Her name is Lillian Files, and in certain circles she's known as The Blue Tornado. She's also known as The Bluebird Lady, because she is totally dedicated to bringing the North American Bluebird back from the edge of extinction.

"I've always been an outdoor person," Lillian explains. "I love to canoe and kayak, and I am very much into wildflowers. I love to gather them in the mornings on the 30 acres surrounding my home in Northern Massachusetts. One day some friends who were visiting said to me, 'Do you know you have a rare bird in your yard?' I admitted I didn't know, and I asked them what it was. They introduced me to my resident bluebirds. Someone even called Massachusetts Audubon Society about it and it wasn't long before

people were driving to my house to catch a glimpse of my rare birds! I wasn't particularly interested in birds at that time, so I had to do some research. That was when I was introduced to the North American Bluebird Society, and my life was changed forever."

Not many types of bird have conservation groups of their own. What's so special about the bluebird? For one thing, they are indigenous only to Canada, the United States and Bermuda. You won't find a bluebird

31

in Europe, or South America. There are three species of bluebirds in North America: the all-blue Mountain Bluebird, the rust-throated Eastern Bluebird, and the blue-throated Western Bluebird, which also has some rust on its back. Sometimes they were called blue robins, because of their ecstatic blue backs, and rusty breasts like the robin. Unlike the robin, their bellies are white, but like the robin, they are part of the thrush family.

Up until the early part of this century, there were plenty of bluebirds in North America. Then came a four-way attack by house sparrows and starlings, DDT, metal fences, and housing developments. House sparrows and starlings were brought to this country from Europe by immigrants who wanted to bring something with them to remind them of their homeland. To make way for new construction, old rotten trees and wooden fence posts were cut down in open fields and meadows, taking the woodpecker holes with them – perfect for bluebirds to nest in – and opening the door for competition (even slaughter) from aggressive birds. Chemicals and insecticides decimated the insect population, destroying the bluebirds' main diet. During the next 40 to 50 years, over 90% of the bluebird population disappeared, placing them on the endangered list in some states.

"You see, bluebirds won't survive without our help," Lillian says. "When I speak to groups, I always ask how many people in the audience have ever seen a bluebird. In the heavily developed areas of Eastern Massachusetts, Rhode Island and Connecticut, I'm lucky if I see two hands go up. Other areas have a little better response rate. People feel an affinity for these family-oriented birds because they exhibit human qualities. They're very approachable birds. If you observe them raising their families, you know their dedication is remarkable. Bluebirds usually have two broods each season, sometimes even three broods. In most bird families, the young go out on their own as soon as they've learned to hunt. On its maiden flight a bluebird nestling can fly as far as 100 feet to a high perch where the male bluebird teaches them to hunt. In bluebird families, the young stay with the parents until they're ready to go south, helping raise the second and third broods, hunting for and bringing food back to their siblings. This is most unusual, and makes people just fall in love with bluebirds!

"The first bluebirds arrive in New England in late February and fly south in mid-October. It's dangerous for them to stay in the north if the winter is warm, because they are insect eaters, and they have to depend on frozen berries in the winter if they don't leave on time, and then they starve. So it's better for them to migrate. It's not unusual for me to have 50 or 60 migrating bluebirds in my yard in mid-October, checking out the housing for the next spring!"

These brilliant harbingers of spring are considered a symbol of love, hope and happiness. Adult birds are only seven inches long, including tail feathers, and their gentle, unassuming nature makes them too timid to fight off the competition from sparrows and starlings, all looking for the same types of nesting spots. The bluebirds' song is a delicate warble, sometimes described as Dear, dear. Think of it, think of it. Lillian's favorite writer, Henry David Thoreau (which she unequivocally states is properly pronounced THUR-o), said that the bluebird carries the sky on its back. He also wrote in 1859: Measure your health by your sympathy with morning and spring. If there is no response in you to the awakening of nature, if the prospect of an early morning walk does not banish sleep, if the warble of the first bluebird does not thrill you – know that the morning and spring of your life are past. Thus may you feel your pulse.

Lillian has learned a great deal from her 20-year affiliation with the North American Bluebird Society, whose 5000 members promote bluebird conservation. "I was so impressed with what people were doing all over the country to establish bluebird trails," she remembers that I came home from my first meeting of the Society in 1978 determined to make a bluebird trail.. A trail is a series of boxes for bluebirds to nest in and can be as short as six boxes. One trail in North Carolina has 2200 boxes, on the edges of golf courses. The Tyngsboro, Massachusetts, trail has 452 boxes. I got so enthused and so involved in saving the bluebirds that the Society asked me to serve on the Board of Directors! After my two years on the board, they asked me to be the President of the Society. How could I say no?"

Over the years, Lillian has given over 460 lectures around New England and serves as trouble shooter throughout the six-state region. She teaches people how to set up bluebird trails and how to protect their birds once they nest. Clearly, bluebirds need all the human help they can get! Lillian gives these hints for would-be bluebird nurturers. "If you have the proper habitat — open fields interspersed with trees and with undergrowth that is not too tall so the birds can spot insects — you can build and place boxes within 25 to 100 feet of a tree or something high for nestlings to fledge to as they don't normally fledge to ground. Bluebirds are very territorial and like to be about 300 feet from their own species. I put up boxes on people's farms or in cemeteries, after I get permission, of course! I used to golf, but that's too slow for me, so the time I spend on golf courses now is to put up bluebird boxes! If you do decide to put up a box or start a trail, you must monitor it. Don't do it unless you can check it at least once a week. Monitoring is really easy. Just make some noise as you approach the box and the female will leave the nest long enough for you to take a quick peek to make sure the babies are okay. (Don't worry! She will come back!) The object is to spot signs of predators (raccoons, snakes, cats, other birds, or blowflies) so you can take steps to protect the nestlings.

"Bluebirds have taken over my life…and I love it! In the spring, it's not unusual for me to get dozens of calls a day from people who have questions about their boxes and their bluebirds. I often joke that I have pediatrician hours: 5:30 A.M. to 11:00 P.M. all day long!

"The bluebirds need us, and we now know what to do for them. We're given this world in trust, and it's our job to take care of it. I'm concerned that so many kids today have no idea what a bluebird is. I'm so glad I only sleep 4 hours a night because there's so much to do! I want to grab every moment I can! I encourage women to live life to the fullest, every single moment of it. Whatever you do, do it with all the enthusiasm and energy you have, and you will make a difference in the world."

Preserving this particular natural treasure is simple and fun, according to Lillian, and her blue eyes sparkle as she issues her challenge. "Not everyone can discover a cure for a deadly disease, or donate millions of dollars to feed the hungry, but anybody can put up a bluebird box and enjoy these gorgeous birds on their property. If you have a bluebird nest on your property, you are one of the chosen ones. I don't know if there is such a thing as reincarnation, but if there is, I want to come back as a bluebird! Twenty years ago, I didn't realize how rare these birds were. Now I can't imagine my life without them."

The bluebirds could easily say the same thing, wondering if they would even be alive without Lillian Files and her fellow bluebird lovers throughout North America!

Susan Duchaine

Building Houses for Women Who Need A Hand Up, Not a Handout

Mother of three boys, Susan Duchaine will probably build close to 60 houses this year. Not all by herself, of course. Susan is the owner and CEO of Design Dwellings in Gorham, Maine, a construction company that specializes in affordable housing.

"By affordable, I mean a house a person can afford to make the payment on after moving in," she explains. "A good portion of my business is in subsidized homes, such as Farmers' Home financed houses. It means a single woman can get into a brand new house for around $300 a month. If she sells the house later, she pays back what she borrowed. And she is able to get her family into a good neighborhood."

Part of Susan's concern for single mothers is because families are very important to her. Her father had a construction business and ten years ago when he began to take life a little easier, Susan started Design Dwellings, Inc. It's been growing ever since. Her brothers own and run Gorham Sand and Gravel, right next door to Design Dwellings.

Not much slows Susan down. She has three boys, ages 7, 8 and 13. When she experienced firsthand the lack of good daycare facilities in her area, she built one. She still owns the property, but sold the business to two women who now run it.

I'm a believer in safety in numbers," Susan explains. "I think daycare facilities can offer a lot, because with 12 or 14 women working in one daycare, there's no chance they will all agree on the right way to do something and that's good. There's less chance for something to go wrong, because one of the 14 would see it.

Her boys like to be on the job with the crew. "They all have streets named after them and they think that's cool," she smiles.

Design Dwellings does a lot of developments. They were just approved for one eleven-lot subdivision, and are at a preliminary stage with 10 more lots, and there are three other subdivisions in various stages of development. That's around 50 lots at the moment.

"I don't just build affordable housing and Farmer's Home subsidized homes," Susan explains. "I've built individual houses in the $250,000 range as well as complete developments. I've even built a veterinary hospital."

Juggling the roles of wife, mother and CEO doesn't bother Susan, unless there's a crisis somewhere. "My kids don't say, 'I don't want to go to school today.' That's never been an option. With two of them, I was back at work when they were two weeks old. With the other one, I took four weeks off. I believe in quality time, not quantity.

"I won't say it's easy. I'm lucky that I had a good day care. That's important, I think, to any working mother. And I have a good husband, which is important to any working mother, too. He's secure in his own identity and working together in the business helps, because we can shuffle the kids easier. When I'm at meetings at night, he can be with the kids, and I do my share, too. We both believe that kids shouldn't be in a day care more than eight or nine hours a day. That's enough for just about anybody, so one of us was always there to pick them up by the end of the day. It makes a big difference. Tim runs the crews, giving me more time to devote to the development end of the business. Before he joined me, I had to do everything!"

How difficult has it been being a woman in a traditionally male business? This woman seems to take it in stride. "I have a good rapport with other builders in the area. (At least I think I do!) Today's buyer is much more educated. For the builder, it's a harder sell, much harder. I think I have a handle on that *because* I'm a woman. I believe I'm more concerned with what's going on than most men. We do everything in our power to get our buyer that house! We probably go over and above more than any other builder out there. We won't dump customers whose deals aren't going well. We work with them.

"Just the other day one of our customers called to say thanks. When we started working with them to build their house, they were turned down because of their debt load. My administrative assistant, Kathy Maurer, worked with them to establish a budget plan. They paid off all their bills and they got a brand new house. The wife is working part time, and they're living on a budget. They called to tell us how great it all is and how happy they are. That's the kind of thing that makes everything worthwhile."

When a customer is turned down or hits a snag in the home building process, Susan and her team can usually come up with some ways to work through the problem. "Most of the time, if they stick with it and follow our lead, we can get them into a house within a year. It may take them a while, but they get there."

There really isn't anything Susan Duchaine doesn't like about the construction business. Being in charge isn't the real turn-on for her, because she believes in giving her people responsibility and the authority to carry it out.

"I've always had vision and foresight," she reflects. "I always seem to know what something's going to look like when it's done. I have this chunk of woods, and all of a sudden, there's a house with parents and kids are living in it. That really is a turn-on for me. Sometimes my customers look at me and say, 'I understand,' and they really don't understand. But after a while, they begin to catch the vision too. I like that end of it. We get thank-you letters from a good portion of them."

Susan is one of nine children. "My whole family has a drive that makes you just want to be out there, involved in everything. I think you have to be born with that. In our family there was no gender-conscious teaching. My parents let us all find our own way. I think that's very important, because there's no reason why women can't do the jobs that men do."

Design Dwellings homes are all stick-built. That means the land is cleared and the foundation is poured and then the framing and finishing area all done on site, by hand. Normally from the day the hole is dug, it's five to six weeks to moving-in day. Susan says, "In nine out of ten houses, we're faster than the banks can process the paperwork. We end up waiting for them. We've got it down to a good system and everyone on the team works extremely well together." It does seem that everyone in the company takes pride in what they do as a team. When you walk in to the beautifully decorated and carefully planned office building, the loyalty and *esprit de corps* almost jump out and shake your hand.

One of Susan's gifts is inspiring her people to give their best effort because their names are on the product. "I want them to make money," she says with a smile. "I don't cut corners on quality and that makes us proud of our work. That keeps us consistent. Each of our houses is built with excellence, whether it's a $95,000 Farmer's Home house for a newly-divorced single mom or a large $250,000 executive home in an exclusive neighborhood."

Even though she's carved out a niche for herself in a tough business, there's a distinctly feminine side to Susan, though she seldom lets it show. She doesn't wear a hard hat to work; she wears slacks and a sweater. Her medium-length blonde hair is softly curled and her makeup is flattering. She admits, "I love my house. I sew and I cook. And I love to shop. That's my favorite! If it's a bad day and I'm nowhere to be found, look for me at a sale!

"Not once in my life have I gotten anything because I am a woman," Susan laughs. "If anything, I've gotten less. I have to jump through more hoops than most men in this business because they never have to convince anyone they can do the job. I hire people strictly for their abilities, not because they're male or female. This past summer I hired a woman who was a finish carpenter who did excellent work for us. I also have a woman draftsperson I hire to draw up the plans. She's top notch and works very well with the customers. That's very important to me because my customers matter to me. I take their wants personally. I care that Jane Doe really wants a cape but can only qualify for a two-bedroom ranch. I know all my customers and they all have a direct link to me. We sell 80% of our own houses, so we really work with the customer from start to finish. We warranty all our work for one year, and we go one step further: We carry a ten-year warranty. That's unusual in this business."

Susan Duchaine is unusual. She even works with the customers on how to keep their homes affordable after they move in: heat costs, taxes, maintenance — all these areas are strategized and are discussed with the customer. After working so hard to get them into the home, the goal is to see them stay in the home.

Design Dwellings doesn't just build homes; they build neighborhoods. Commitment, integrity, loyalty and hard work have built Susan's business. It isn't always easy being a woman in construction, but a sense of humor helps. One road she built is called Easy Street, not because they made a lot of money on it, but because it was easy to build.

The word quit is not in Susan Duchaine's vocabulary. She believes people can do anything they put their minds to. But her steely determination and spunk are tempered by her concern and compassion. She consistently demonstrates her commitment to family values and good honest work by extending herself and her company to people who need and deserve a helping hand over the pitfalls of building a first house. What she's building is not just a house; it's a place to call home.

She is quite modest about her random acts of kindness. About seven years ago, her brother was in the hospital after being severely burned. A young boy, more severely burned than her brother, caught Susan's attention and compassion. When she learned a new addition would be needed to his family's home in order to accommodate his handicap, Susan called United Way to see if she could help. Because the family lived in a mobile home that was in need of repair, Susan and her people built an entire house. "Subcontractors worked, my crew worked, I worked, and a lot of other people worked. Incidentals were paid for, and the lumber was donated by a local building supply company. I certainly didn't do it alone. Together, we made a difference."

Another woman who had shot and killed her estranged husband in self defense when he burst into the house and threatened to kill them came to Susan for help. After acquittal, the woman and her children needed to start over in a new location. Susan helped them get a new house and a fresh start. There are dozens more examples of Susan's generosity and kindness that are known only to the people she's helped and her loyal staff and crew. It's enough for Susan to know that she's been able to help people fulfill their great American dream: a home of their own.

41

Jeannette Clift George

Taking Center Stage to Warn Young People about Substance Abuse

From a strong, stubborn Dutch watchmaker imprisoned in a vermin-infested Nazi concentration camp to a sweet, innocent Alice in the fantasy world of Wonderland, Jeannette Clift George has portrayed women of strength and insight on film and on stage.

"I was very shy as I grew up in Houston, Texas, although you'd never guess that now!" Jeannette laughs. "By the time I entered college, I knew I wanted to act. We all have women in our lives who make a profound impression on us, and one of mine was my college drama teacher, Maude Adams. Miss Adams was a well known actress who, in her retirement, chose to be a drama instructor at Stephens College. She taught me some wonderful things – about acting, about life, and about being a woman in the world of the theater. I was so impressionable that I would have followed any pattern placed before me, and I'm very glad she  was the one who was instrumental in shaping my career. She was a great role model for me, especially because she was also shy. I remember one opening night when I was so nervous I tried to hide in a large broom closet in the theater just to calm down. I opened the door, and there was Miss

Adams! We looked at each other in shock, and then she asked if I'd like to sit down. So I did! We didn't even talk to each other! I still remember sitting in that closet with my drama teacher, each of us gaining strength from the other's presence. Of course, the show opened on schedule and we both did what was expected of us."

After earning her degree in drama from the University of Texas, Jeannette moved to New York City. After fifteen years of the usual run of various off-Broadway theater pieces, and summer stock, she was hired to be one of the ensemble actors at the Alley Theater in Houston (one of the top theaters in the country). The Ford Foundation had conducted a survey of regional theaters around the country and had determined that they could not survive on their box office sales alone, so they were recruiting professional actors from the east and west coasts to add strength and drawing power. Jeannette was approached and accepted the challenge, moving back to Houston to act at The Alley Theater.

In her off-stage life, she was asked to teach acting classes at what is now Houston Baptist University. Always searching for plays with a spiritual dimension to add a new layer of depth to her career, she formed an experimental group for her students to try their hand at improvisation. "We became an independent theater, which I called The After Dinner Players, because I thought someone would feed us and then we'd put on a play for them!" Jeannette remembers.

Now known simply as the A.D. Players, the group is one of the few theaters in the country that has a program for interns. Students come from California, Idaho, Oklahoma and Switzerland to gain drama experience and be nurtured. "We have anywhere from six to ten interns interested in a career in the theater arts," says Jeannette, "and they are not all actors. This year we have a costuming intern, for example. By the time they leave the A.D. Players at the end of the nine months, they will have experienced every aspect of theater: lighting, set building, costuming, and box office sales. It's the equivalent training of a graduate level degree in theater. Not only is it fun and rewarding for me to work with these young people, it's my way of helping my profession, just as someone invested time and effort in me when I was a new actor. My interest has always been in young people and students," she says. "This company is a way of equipping our future actors. Some go on to form their own companies.

Some go into grad school. Some go on to professional theater."

One very special commitment Jeannette has made is to educate America's young people about substance abuse through the theater arts. "Our company goes into both public and private schools with a program addressing drug and chemical abuse through special drug information assemblies all over the country," she explains. "Theater touches lives in a way no lecture or pamphlet could ever achieve. The audience identifies with the characters on the stage, and the message hits home: chemical abuse is not the way out of your problems. It only drags you further down."

In 1975, Jeannette was asked to audition for a part in the movie The Hiding Place, the story of one incredibly strong Dutch family who were imprisoned for helping Jews escape Nazi persecution during World War II. The Ten Boom family built a hidden room in their home and assisted Jews fleeing the country. The film is the story of Corrie, the eldest daughter, and follows her through her horrific ordeal and miraculous survival.

"I was asked to audition for the part of Katia, the prisoner who befriended Corrie and her sister, Betsy (played by Julie Harris). I rushed out to buy a copy of the book, and there was no Katia in it! How was I supposed to prepare for that part?" Jeannette laughs. "At the audition, the producers assured me Katia would be in the movie, so I read for the role and went home to wait for the casting decision. I knew several big name actresses were being considered for the role of Corrie, including Ingrid Bergman, who had a schedule conflict and couldn't do it. When I was asked to play the part of Corrie, I was completely overwhelmed. The thought of making my film debut in a part of such magnitude was frightening. I was in the habit of turning such decisions over to God and followed what I believed to be His direction. In retrospect, I know acting that part in that movie was one of the grandest opportunities of my life."

Anyone who has seen The Hiding Place senses that Jeannette is more than acting a part when, as Corrie, she tells how the love of God sustains a person even in the most horrifying of circumstances. There is a reality in her eyes that is at the same time both great acting and something much more; her own convictions and faith leap off the screen, inspiring the minds and hearts of the audience. At those times, she is Corrie Ten Boom,

45

and no one could think she is merely acting a part. Granted, in her own personal life she has not suffered to the extent those women suffered in Ravensbruck Concentration Camp, but her credibility is strong because of her own deep convictions and commitment to God. She is not just speaking Corrie's words; she is sharing her own faith. This was more than casting genius on the part of the filmmaker.

"It really surprised me that I received so much recognition and so many awards after my role as Corrie," she says. "I found myself faced with a decision: stay in films and build a career on the basis of the recognition I was getting, or go home to Houston. I had recently married, The A.D. Players was newly formed and Houston offered the option of continuing my performing career on stage. It was a definite decision that directed my life into the activity I now follow. I feel I made the right choice. It's our prerogative to question choices and learn from them, but if we carry the heaviness of regret for the choices we've made, we lose the value of the past and miss the celebration of the present. Choices in the past get us where we are, but choices in the present put the past to good use. I enjoy doing what I do."

Under Jeannette's direction, The A.D. Players run two theaters consecutively, producing ten shows a season. Jeannette writes many of them. The full variety of theater is offered in Grace Theater, their main stage. The shows in the Rotunda theater, provided by Houston's St. Luke's Methodist Church, are especially tailored for children with the audience volunteers performing in many of the scenes. This increases the children's appreciation of theater and the culture it represents. With emphasis on television and films, many young people have become bystanders and live theater encourages participation in the action. All of the plays have messages of encouragement or education. Jeannette's adaptation of Alice in Wonderland, for example, had an emphasis on encouraging children to read. She has recently published, Daisy Petals, a book of inspirational thoughts. She also has a daily radio program of short, inspirational insights called, Jeannette Clift George from Center Stage.

For her thirty years of work as administrative and artistic director of her professional theater company, Jeannette Clift George was honored in 1997 by Rotary International with the Jean Harris Award, given to women who further the cause of women. She acknowledges that her love of God permeates all of her work. "I believe that theater's highest assignment is to speak to the soul and to encourage the enlightenment and elevation of the human spirit to its full place," she states. "This is a challenge I have accepted. I also believe laughter is part of that assignment, so we have a lot of laughter in our work at A.D. Players. Life isn't always solemn. God has a sense of humor, too!"

This deeply spiritual, refreshingly humble woman has a word of encouragement for women everywhere. "Be assured of who you are as a woman. If you want to be an architect, be a woman who is an architect! There is so much pressure on us to be people we are not! If we become who we are not to get to where we want to go, the person we are will never make the trip! I've learned there's nothing more aggravating to insecurity than success. If you've abandoned yourself, success means nothing. Live your life center stage. This doesn't mean being self-centered. It means making active choices, and being a participant in your own life. In the theater we say, The past got me here, but I don't live in the past. I live this present moment."

Vivian Castleberry

Pioneering Journalism and World Peace

Trying things that other women didn't usually do was normal for Vivian Castleberry. "I believe women usually make great strides and come into their own when there are great crises in the world. I was raised during the Great Depression," she explains, "but we always had plenty to eat because we were a farm family and we produced our own food. I came of age during World War II. I remember sitting on the gym floor with the other students at Southern Methodist University, listening to the radio as President Roosevelt asked Congress to declare a state of war with Japan after the bombing of Pearl Harbor. I was a journalism student and had known all my life that I would be a writer. When you have printer's ink in your blood, you just cannot help being drawn to where the action is!"

After college, Vivian launched her journalism career at the largest oil publication in the country, The Petroleum Engineer, in Dallas, Texas. "It was a very boring job!" she laughs. "I'm a people person, and there I was, an editorial assistant (really a glorified gofer) dealing with things instead of people. But it was great training! My boss was from an Oklahoma oil family, and she was a taskmaster. As a result, I learned the discipline it takes to be available when a story breaks, and the long hours necessary to

49

do a complete job to report the whole story. My mother had taught me to ask questions and to be thorough. That lesson is still paying off."

Vivian graduated from high school in the same class as Curtis Castleberry. Although they never dated, they corresponded with each other the entire three and a half years he was serving as a Marine in the South Pacific. "It was a small town and we were friends," she says. "I corresponded with a lot of young men, because I thought it was my patriotic duty! It was something special with Curt. We fell in love by letter. I was a good correspondent. Even today I write letters rather than fax or pick up the phone! Some things don't change!"

Curt and Vivian were married in 1946. The first two years were an extended honeymoon. "It was absolutely glorious!" she remembers. "I helped him spend everything he had saved!" Realizing that his career was not going to advance without a college degree, Curt enrolled at Texas A&M. Women were not allowed as students. Typically optimistic and enterprising, Vivian spotted an opportunity where there was none and became the first women's editor of the daily newspaper: the Texas A&M Battalion, also the town paper. "I haunted the offices until they created a job for me," she laughs. "I covered the city council, as well as college news. It gave me an opportunity to hone my skills and prepare for the next rung of the career ladder."

Always needing an intellectual challenge, Vivian encouraged Curt to move back to Dallas. She went back to her old job for eighteen months. While she was on maternity leave with her third child, the Dallas Times Herald called and asked her to accept a position as home editor, covering home furnishings, interior design and decorating. "What I knew about this subject was minuscule," she says. "But it was a way to get my toe in the door. I started out in a hurry, and made my job into what I wanted it to be. I retired from the paper 28 years later."

Determined to put her own spin on her assignment, Vivian wrote a series of articles, called Homemaking Under Handicap, for which she won a state-wide writing award. "I didn't focus on decorating. Instead, I keyed the stories to people who had created happy home environments under extreme handicap. Again, my focus was on people, rather than on things.

"When I found out I was pregnant with our fourth child, I bought into the thinking of that time that I couldn't raise four kids and have a full-time career. So, I resigned my position as home editor. The day I came home from the hospital with my new baby, one of my favorite editors at the paper called and asked if I would return as women's editor. I went through a tremendous inner struggle, wondering how I could raise my children and still have the career I wanted so very much. Curt freed me to take the job, promising that he and the children would be copartners on the home front.

"As women's editor, my hours were endless. I managed a staff of twelve, made assignments, determined what would be included every day, oversaw page layouts, made countless speeches in the community representing the paper. And I continued to go on assignments and to write. I told my paper I would not take the job if I could not continue to be a reporter as well as the editor. We published a section daily except Saturday, two Sunday sections and a weekly food section that sometimes ran as much as 30 pages.

"From the outset, I convinced my bosses that even though I could do their job amazingly well, I had to have some leniency in scheduling my time. I said I could not afford to foul up at home and they could not afford to have a women's editor who did. I had to be inclusive. Sometimes the kids went with me to the office on Sunday afternoons, doing their homework while I worked. When I became pregnant with our fifth child, I took a leave of absence, the first woman at the paper allowed to do so. For many years I was the only woman in a position of responsibility. Eventually I was named to the editorial board, the sacrosanct part of the newspaper.

"In my lifetime women have made some progress. We still have a long way to go. I covered in depth the second wave of the women's movement in America. I was there when Betty Friedan published The Feminine Mystique and I covered Gloria Steinem and the beginning of Ms Magazine. I interviewed office holders and every president's wife from Bess Truman to Lady Bird Johnson. I covered the Kennedy assassination. Sooner or later, everybody who was anybody came to Dallas and I covered most of them."

Vivian is particularly happy about one series of articles she wrote called The Good Marriage. In a Dallas speech, the president of American Marriage Counselors said that after ten years of marriage, most couples were not happy. Vivian set out to discover what comprised a happy marriage. She sent a letter and a questionnaire to 100 couples whose names she secured from clergymen and other professionals, citing the remark and asking them to return the questionnaire if they agreed they had a happy marriage. Fifty-seven responses were returned, most of them from both husband and wife. The overwhelming response was that, for them, marriage got better as time went by. "Curt and I can vouch for that," she says. "We've been married 51 years and it's marvelous! I think it's time that those of us who are in great relationships stand up and be counted!"

Feeling that she had done all she could do at the newspaper, Vivian took a five-week vacation with her husband. "I didn't wear makeup, lived in jeans, and walked the streams and mountains in Colorado, communed with my God and listened to my inner voice. I was determined to find out who I was in addition to what I did! I came home and told my family I would retire in two years. My daughters were placing bets on whether or not I would really retire!" Retire she did, leaving the paper, resigning from all responsibilities in the community and moving 100 miles away from Dallas. "I knew I was retiring to something, not from something," she said.

"If you ever hang it up, you've lost it!" Vivian laughs. "Every day you need to pick up the new challenge and tell yourself this is, indeed, the first day of the rest of my life! That is what is making the retirement years the richest part of my life. After I retired as a working journalist, I took all the material I had accumulated and wrote Daughters of Dallas: A History of the Greater Dallas Community, Concentrating on the Gifts and Talents of Its Women. It was published in June 1994 and spans 150 years of Dallas history, from the arrival of the first woman in 1842 to the first woman mayor, Annette Strauss in 1992 (for whom Vivian campaigned).

While she was in the process of retiring, one of Vivian's friends, Sharon Tennison, came to visit. She had been doing some speaking under the auspices of Physicians for Social Responsibility about the medical consequences of nuclear war, and had decided to go see the Russian people for herself. She asked Vivian to go along on the second trip to Russia, Vivian said no. "I didn't want to go. This was Sharon's thing, not my thing!" Sharon planned the entire trip from Vivian's home. After hearing the phone conversations, and watching the trip come together, Vivian was hooked. She went to Russia. "It was a wonderful experience," she enthuses. We were in three different cities, meeting individuals in their homes and visiting colleges and universities. At the University of Moscow, I discovered an immediate rapport with one of the professors, Dr. Lily Golden. As we said goodbye, Lily said, 'Men have been trying to bring about peace for 100 years and they haven't made much progress. Go home and bring us your women.' I was moved, but honestly didn't think I'd do anything. Then Sharon called. She had been invited by the Soviet Women's Committee to bring a group of women in leadership from the United States to Moscow and Leningrad to talk to their women about how we manage our lives. She asked me to help. I said no. When I told my husband, he just grinned at me and asked when I was going to call her back and tell her I would do it."

Vivian began writing to women in leadership positions, starting with the President's wife and Justice Sandra Day O'Connor, inviting them to go to Russia. She and Sharon contacted women who had a key interest in bringing about a peaceful resolution to human conflict. Most of them declined. But the seeds were being planted

In the midst of this, one of Vivian's friends, Dolores Pevehouse, called and said, "There is something you must do!" That something was almost exactly what Lily had challenged Vivian to do. In 1986, Vivian invited 12 close friends to her home to discuss forming an organization to cultivate that seed Lily had planted and Dolores cultivated: getting women together to discuss ways they could promote world peace. In 1987, Vivian took a group to Russia without Sharon. When she returned, she was serious about world peace. The group she had pulled together in 1986 became the core of Peacemakers, Inc. Its mission: to sponsor a world-wide peace conference for women.

In August of 1988, 2000 women (as well as a lot of men) from 37 of the 50 states, and 63 countries, met in Dallas for one week to discuss ways of bringing about global peace. Every continent was represented. "We spent a full week talking about how we as women can create a more peaceful world in which to rear our children," Vivian recalls. "It was a life-changing event."

After the conference, the committee voted itself into a board and they have continued to work. Delegates to the 8/8/88 conference have kept in touch. The next Peacemakers conference is planned for 9/9/99. It seems fitting – a good close to the old millennium and a good start to the new one.

Vivian Castleberry has received many awards and honors, including being named one of the change agents for the coverage of women's news in America by *The Washington Press Club Foundation*. She helped *found The Women's Center of Dallas*, the *Dallas Women's Foundation*, and the *Women's Issues Network*, and served on the advisory board for the founding *of The Family Place*, the first sanctuary for battered women in Dallas. She also served on the advisory committee for Southern Methodist University's *Symposium on the Education of Women for Social and Political Leadership*, now in its 34th year. She was named the *Texas Mother of the Year* in 1996. She is slated to chair the 1998 *Power of Positive Parenting Conference* under the auspices of American Mothers, Inc. Clearly, the word *retirement* means something different to Vivian than it does to the rest of the world!

"I believe each woman has a responsibility to chart her own course. If I could sit down with every woman in the world, one on one, my message would be the same to each: *Never stop.* I used to think I would eventually reach the stage of life when I'd have it all together. I learned some time ago, that people who do that are the most miserable in the world. They stop at the peak of their careers and retire. They think they've reached the millennium. But if you gift wrap your life and put it on the shelf and it collects dust, you die. I know I'll *never* have it all together. And that's okay. That's living!"

From a reporter's standpoint, tomorrow's story is the only important thing. With Vivian Castleberry, whatever tomorrow's story is, it's certain to be awesomely inspiring.

Major Pearl Asperschlager

Living the Spirit of Christmas 365 Days a Year

Turkeys, toys and tambourines are a normal part of life for Pearl Asperschlager during the holidays. She and her husband, Gary, are both majors in the Salvation Army and they administer the many social and spiritual phases of the work in Old Orchard Beach, Maine. It's a whole lot more than red kettles and a whole lot more than just on Sundays. For Pearl, and the many volunteers of the Salvation Army, keeping (and giving away) the Christmas spirit is a way of life.

"Like most people," Pearl says, "my only impression of the Salvation Army was the red kettles at Christmas time, because that is what's visible. When I learned more about it, what interested me was that the work went beyond normal church activities and met the needs of people on a daily basis...not just on Sundays."

What makes a young woman in her junior year of college decide to postpone her education to visit nursing homes and preach on street corners? Pearl explains, "I believe God has a plan for our lives where we can best be used and feel fulfilled at the same time. I just asked God what I should do with my life and this is where I was led. I have just one life and I wanted to make it count. I've been very happy and fulfilled, and have not had any doubts or regrets. I'm in the right place."

Pearl's first commission as an Officer was to be sent to open a new Salvation Army Corps among one small group of people with an Appalachian-type culture on top of a mountain in New Jersey. Her mandate was to hold Sunday services, Sunday school, and youth activities as well as continue the tutorial program that was already in effect. In addition, she was to start a summer day camp program for the children and get the parents involved. "I was there by myself three of the four years. Every day it was daunting to think about starting something new and realize what a responsibility I had been given. But I do like a challenge! And good things kept happening. One day, a Princeton Seminary student with this very strange last name called and said that he was supervising a group of young people and asked if I could use any help on Sundays. Every other Sunday for a whole year he brought a group of 20 teenagers up on the mountain and helped me start the Sunday school. Things went well, for both the project and for us. Four years later, we were married."

The Salvation Army has a variety of programs to meet people at all levels of need, from the most basic of food, clothing, and shelter, to education and drug rehabilitation. They also have character-building activities such as girls' and boys' programs equivalent to Girl Scouts and Brownies or Boy Scouts and Cub Scouts. Music is a very important part of the program, so children learn to play instruments.

"Some people may not know that the Salvation Army is a church," Pearl explains. "Each congregation is called a Corps. This Corps has a full range of community programs. We have case work services where we help people, mostly with food. Each person requesting help is interviewed. Unfortunately, we can't spend as much time as we'd like with each person. Sometimes, you wonder if it's a band-aid or if you're really helping. The same people keep coming back again and again. They don't seem to be moving on with their lives, and you don't know quite how to help them. Fortunately we have a good network of support services and we can do a lot of referrals. We work with other welfare directors, community action programs and food pantries. We don't work independently of other agencies; we all work together.

"Monies are clearly defined for one purpose or another and we use all contributions with integrity. We're part of United Way, but that doesn't mean we have to compromise our basic motivation: working to meet the needs of the *whole* person, including spiritual needs. If the situation warrants, our secretary will invite people to come to our programs and services. But we certainly don't make it a prerequisite for getting any help. If the opportunity arises and that need presents itself, we make the invitation." But the help is never dependent upon their participating in church events. For anyone who is alone or homeless, or indigent, there is a feeding program three days a week right in the gymnasium. People make a small donation if they're able. If they're not, that's fine too. At the holiday season, both Thanksgiving and Christmas dinners are served. Sometimes people need help putting together a big holiday dinner in their own homes. Last year this Corps gave 150 families each a bag or two of groceries to cook a holiday dinner. The food baskets are packed by volunteer help from a local bank and a school. Pearl suggests that it is a good idea to call before showing up to volunteer at any Corps, since needs vary from day to day.

She explains other outreaches. "Here we have an extensive nursing home visitation program where our folks conduct church services monthly, and spend time visiting and passing out gifts. At Christmas time we visit 10 to 12 nursing homes to give a Christmas remembrance to all the residents. We buy these gifts with contributed funds.

"We also have a toy shop where parents can choose toys for their children. Every year my garage is filled with toys donated by a local motorcycle club. You know, toys used to be able to be fixed, but that's not true anymore. We can't fix a Nintendo or plastic toy. If people are going to donate, they need to give new things and nice things that they would give to their own children. Unfortunately, we can't repair broken toys. We don't have the facilities, or the time, or the ability. It's counterproductive for us to have to take unsuitable or broken toys to the dump.

"The local Coats for Kids program enables us to give a coat to every person who comes in the door during the winter months. Last year we distributed 4,000 coats in our area alone. This is a state-wide program sponsored by WCSH-TV, Shaw's and Pratt-Abbott Cleaners for the Salvation Army. The TV station publicizes the program, the grocery stores collect the coats, and the dry cleaner cleans all the coats and gives them to Salvation Army facilities to distribute locally. When a person comes in for any kind of assistance, we can give them not just the food, and not just toys for the children, but also a warm coat for everybody in the family. It's a wonderful program that people can feel very good about.

"The red donation boxes you see around the area are for good used items. The Adult Rehabilitation Centers do the collection and those items are resold in our thrift stores to support the drug and alcohol rehabilitation centers in large cities. There is a residential program of recovery that people can be involved in. Part of it is work therapy such as driving a truck, picking up donations, working in the stores, or in the sorting room. And there is that other aspect of the help we offer, the spiritual aspect, that perhaps isn't there in other community programs."

What about the red kettles? During the Depression in the 1920s, the Salvation Army was hard hit, like everyone else. With Christmas coming, they didn't know how they were going to help people. Going directly to the public with the red kettles was the answer. Now it's one of the most visible symbols of the Salvation Army. One year in one area, over $50,000 was raised from the red kettles alone. The majority of it is used at holiday time, but it all gets used eventually because assistance is provided all year long. The local Corps supports itself and gives money above and beyond that to support the community programs. Money contributed by the community always goes back into the community.

Pearl doesn't see herself as being that different from other working mothers. "We have three teenagers and we are very careful to maintain a normal family life. Our children are a part of all that we do, but we are very careful to balance our life in such a way that our own children don't get short-changed. We make the same kind of balances in our home life as other families do when both parents work. For us, *full-time* often includes evenings as well as all day. Of course, Sunday is a work day in our household!"

From its beginning in 1865, the Salvation Army has always given women the privilege of being officers. There don't seem to be any power trips or identity crises in the Asperschlager household. Pearl and her husband are both commissioned individually as ordained ministers. There is an unmistakable twinkle in Pearl's eye when she says, "I'm not the minister's wife. There are *two* ministers here." Due in part to the efforts of retired General Eva Burrows (a single Australian woman who served as head of the denomination for seven years) The Salvation Army is now in 95 countries, including Russia and Eastern Europe.

How does Pearl Asperschlager stay so calm with all those irons in the kettle? She responds, "I think God gives you a sense of peace as you are doing what you are meant to do. Everyday is a different challenge, and everyday I ask God to direct me to the right person or the right priorities for the day because there's always more to do than you can ever accomplish, there are always more needy people than you can help. You can put your mind to this group of people, but in 10 minutes, you're going to get a call to think about something else. So it's a balancing act all the time. I spend a lot of time at my desk, because administration needs to be done and I have a gift for it. We have a lot of volunteers and I work with the leaders of the programs to enable them. It's a different kind of a life, that a lot of people might not be able to relate to, but I see it as an adventure."

A spirit of adventure together with a strong faith and a compassionate heart make Major Pearl Asperschlager an inspiration to everyone she meets. It is because of her commitment to excellence and her servant's attitude that life is made easier for the thousands of families in her care.

Ja'nette Agosto

Educating Kids about AIDS

She's 16, going on 40, with a wisdom beyond her years, and she's the youngest certified AIDS educator in the State of Maine. Poised and slender, Ja'nette Agosto is a marvelous mixture of feisty young woman unwilling to tolerate prejudice and ignorance, and normal teenager describing how she's going to wear her hair to the next dance. But something is definitely wrong with this picture. A kid shouldn't have to be this old at sixteen.

Ja'nette's mom, Terry Dannemiller, got HIV from her husband, and died of AIDS on August 1, 1993. And Ja'nette's sister, Autum Aquino got HIV from Terry as an infant, drawing blood by biting while she was nursing, and swallowing some blood along with her mother's milk. Terry hadn't known then that she was HIV positive.

Suddenly, Ja'nette Agosto grew up. "I sensed that something was wrong when my mom started withdrawing from me emotionally," Ja'nette says. "But I thought I had done something wrong and she was upset with me. As it went on and didn't get better, I really began to worry. Then Mom told me she had learned she had AIDS and was going to die in a little while. Then I understood why she was acting differently.

She was trying to protect me. But it just made me think I had done something wrong, and I was very relieved to learn that I had nothing to do with what was happening to her. It didn't make the situation any easier to take, but at least I could help her and be strong for her. After that, Mom and I were closer than ever."

Before Terry died, she and her two girls went to live with her sister and brother-in-law. After her death, the girls made their home with their Aunt Lynn and Uncle Brad. Terry and Lynn grew up in an abusive situation and Lynn left home at 12 to live with her father. Terry married at 15. They lived apart, but they always stayed close emotionally. When Lynn married Brad and they discovered they couldn't have children of their own, the sense of family became even more important in all their lives. "Terry and I always knew one of us would have a child named Autum, Lynn smiles. "It was the most logical step for the girls to live with us after Terry died."

"If it weren't for Aunt Lynn and Uncle Brad," Ja'nette shakes her head as she unconsciously reaches out to caress her little sister's arm, "Autum and I would be separated. They make it possible for us to be a family. Not everyone is this lucky."

From the energetic greeting of the two Schnauzers to the quiet, strong man who comes home from his mail carrier route late afternoons, everything testifies that life in this home is full of love. Difficult situations seem to have brought out the best in these people who talk about life and death and school dances and what's for dinner in the same conversation. What gives people such grace in the face of personal disaster?

Ja'nette talks about Terry's legacy. "My mom was a terrific woman. She had a hilarious sense of humor. She was the favorite mom among all my friends. I always had friends staying with me, even when I was grounded! She didn't mind the extra mouths to feed because at least she knew where I was and that I was okay. I was very, very close to my mom, and when she found out she had AIDS, we got even closer. I'm still close to her, even though she died."

The September 1993 issue of *The Scoop*, published by the People With Aids Coalition of Maine, paid this tribute to Terry: Theresa (Terry) Wade Dannemiller was a woman of vision who could see things others never dreamed of. A woman of courage who stood for what she believed in regardless of the cost. A caring woman who touched hearts, changed minds and saved lives. A tiny woman in high heels with a Pepsi in one hand, a big grin and the determination of a bulldog. A mother, laughing with her children and her family, who spent her time and energy teaching us to be strong in spirit, to speak boldly against injustice, to teach one another and to work together to make the world a safer, more accepting place for persons living with AIDS." She was one month shy of being 30 years old when she died.

What made Ja'nette decide to become an AIDS educator? "The summer after I finished third grade I started to ask questions because my mom kept dropping hints. She pushed me away a lot [emotionally] when she first found out she had AIDS. She'd ask, "What do you think is really wrong with Autum?" But the big tip-off to me was when she would answer the phone calls from PWAs (People With AIDS) and she didn't think I was listening. I was pretty certain she had AIDS and I just *had* to talk to someone about it. So I told my best friend. I just needed to let it out. One day my mom said, 'Do you want to tell other kids about it, since you haven't had a chance?' I froze up, and she knew I had told someone. 'Well,' she said, 'let's just see what happens.' What happened was the word got out, but by that time, Terry and Ja'nette were ready to go public with the story. People reacted out of ignorance and lack of information, because they were not so well educated as today.

Ja'nette gave a speech to the kids at her school about AIDS when she was in fourth grade. By the time she was in seventh grade, she was certified as an AIDS educator, the youngest one in the state. To be certified to educate people about AIDS (Acquired Immune Deficiency Syndrome), Ja'nette had to attend a day-long course. "And, oh, is it a *long* day!" she remembers. "You tell your own story and you role play and you learn what language is appropriate and what language is inappropriate. You have to get comfortable with speaking in front of an audience and with answering their questions. You have to keep your temper, no matter what.

"My mom was both a sex educator and AIDS educator. One time someone in an audience said to her, *You should be shot like an in-bred cat! How could you do this to your child?* Mom never lost her temper. She just quietly replied, 'There's no need for that.' and went on with her talk."

AIDS is a disease you can get form body fluids: through blood transfusions or bleeding wounds, from unprotected sex, or from sharing needles. You can't get it from saliva, or hugging, or shaking hands with a person with AIDS or with someone carrying the virus. You can't get it by using toilets, sinks, bathtubs, or swimming pools that a person infected with the AIDS virus has used. You can't get it by using dishes, utensils, or food handled by a person infected with the AIDS virus. And you can't get it by being near sneezing, coughing or spitting by a person infected with the virus. The AIDS virus is not spread by casual contact.

AIDS with its flu-like symptoms has been around a long time, but they didn't name it until around 1985. "It makes you wonder," reflects Ja'nette, "when you hear about all the people who died of influenza 50 years ago if it was really influenza or AIDS with a name."

How has AIDS affected Autum? Lynn says, "She gets the normal childhood diseases, but she's not sick more often than most children with AIDS. She's had chicken pox several times. The first time, they call it chicken pox. After that, it's called shingles. She's had it eight times."

Autum and her family made the local news when Terry decided to move to Florida in order to improve their quality of life and protect the girls from people who didn't understand the situation and, out of ignorance, were making life more difficult than it had to be.

To look at Autum now, you'd never guess she had AIDS. Beautiful dark eyes and hair testify to her Hispanic heritage, and her bubbly enthusiasm for life spills over to everyone she meets. It's impossible to meet Autum and not smile. Life seems very normal in her presence. When posing for a recent photo, suddenly Autum grinned at Ja'nette and blurted out, "You were *hatched!*" "And you came from a cabbage patch!" Ja'nette laughs back.

Perfectly normal conversation between two sisters, hiding the deep love between them. When she was two, Autum was diagnosed with AIDS. Now she is a 12-year old, doing her asthma therapy like any normal kid with asthma. She is one of the oldest children with AIDS. "Everybody wants to be Autum's friend, Ja'nette says with obvious pride. "She's very sociable and makes friends easily. Her self esteem is *very* healthy! She loves her name, and grew up thinking the season and all the leaves are named after her!"

Lynn adds, "We taught the girls to love themselves. Terry and I boosted each other's self esteem all the time when we were growing up. If I could give one message it would be that mothers belong on Earth, not in Heaven. Protect yourself for your kids." Autum adds with a smile, "Aunt Lynn and Mom were almost like twins when they were growing up." Ja'nette nods her agreement. "My mom had a very, very bad childhood. Mom knew if she didn't make it happen for herself, no one else was going to do it for her. She would tell people, "Take charge of your life and protect yourself. You have to love yourself. It's your life and you have to take care of it."

There's a lot of normalcy in this family. Lynn says, "Ja'nette is very smart. She loses patience with things that take a long time. Terry, Brad and I have raised the kids together. We called it *co-parenting*." In spite of the normalcy, every so often the reality of AIDS settles over them. Sometimes a kid will call Ja'nette an unkind name. She doesn't tolerate it. To quote her, "I just say, 'Ex*cuse* me! My mom died from a disease you get from sex. I don't think you know what you're talking about.' I get into it with some of them once in a while. They're just being kids. More often they won't think and they'll make a joke about AIDS and then they'll immediately say, 'Oh! Sorry, sorry! What have I said!' They're almost all sensitive to the situation. If they're not sensitive, they're just ignorant."

Ja'nette has had some very understanding teachers. Both Autum and Ja'nette have close friends who lend support and keep life normal for them. "When I was younger," Ja'nette says, "I wasn't allowed to be around other kids because my mom always worried about my exposure to prejudice. She worried that when others found out she had AIDS, I would pay the price emotionally. I was in fourth grade before I attended my first sleep-over. I was always around adults. When something like this happens to you, you just can't help but grow up fast. I'd hear about kids piercing each other's belly buttons and ear and wonder, *Why would you want to do that? Don't you know you can get HIV that way?* I can be very serious about the things that really matter in life."

Ja'nette has a tough message for teenagers: "There's no guy hot enough and there's no girl cute enough to have to wake up every morning and realize you're going to die because of one stupid mistake, even if he or she says, 'But I love you!' If you have sex with someone, you trust your life

65

to him or her. It's like playing Russian roulette. You don't want to do it, believe me. So wait for sex. If you can't do that, at least use protection. Peer pressure is tough. You don't want to wake up every morning and look in the mirror and say, 'I've got AIDS and I'm going to die and I *could* have stopped it.' You don't want to live with that regret.

"I was twelve when Mom died. The most important thing is to love your parents. Don't say or think or do bad things, because you never know when you're going to lose them. If you do lose them, you're going to feel really guilty about what you said or did. You never know what you have – until it's gone."

Autum's prognosis is very good right now. The AIDS is lying dormant. "I want to be a nurse when I grow up," Autum says as she draws a smiley face on a clipboard. Then she adds dark curly hair, like hers, and signs her name beautifully. Then Ja'nette takes the pen, draws two musical notes and a shoe with a high heel and signs her name beneath them. She wants to be a criminal law prosecutor. She's an honor student, and has many friends who support her and believe in her. "It has been five years since Mom died and I now know that, no matter what, I'll make it!" Anyone who knows her, has no doubt of that!

Marian Adair

Building Bridges of International Understanding

Tipper Gore belongs. So does Alma Powell, Colin Powell's wife. Three presidents' wives — Ladybird Johnson, Barbara Bush, and Betty Ford have all belonged as well. Their lives were enriched and changed because of their membership. Thanks to one woman from Fort Wayne, Indiana: Marian Adair.

Remember what it's like to be the new kid on the block? Not only do you not know anyone, no one takes the initiative to get to know you! You know it won't last because you'll make friends eventually, but those first few weeks can be very lonely.

In 1953 Marian and Ross Adair were new in Washington. Ross had been elected to the U.S. House of Representatives, and the family moved to Washington, D.C. "Living in D.C. is both an exhilarating and daunting experience," Marian explains. "When you're new, you try so hard to maintain a normal life for your family, but you have all the rules of politics and protocol to think about. Some things you wouldn't hesitate to do in your home town, you wouldn't even dare to think about in Washington! For example, the  wife of a new representative would never call the wife of an ambassador by her first name. Nor would you speak to the wife of a supreme court justice unless she spoke to you first. It just isn't done! Protocol moves Washington. It's a very different way of life.

"At a dinner party, for example, people are seated according to rank. Not long after we arrived in Washington, we were invited to the French Embassy for a black tie dinner. It was unusual for us junior people to be invited and we were eager to make a good first impression. When we had moved our family to Washington, we had bought a new contraption called a television. (You have to remember this was 1950 and we were from Ft. Wayne, Indiana, where there were no television channels!). Our children, Carol and Stevie, were 11 and 7 and of course, they loved the TV. In those days, we felt fairly comfortable leaving them in front of the TV with neighbors nearby when we had to go out for the evening. The night of the dinner at the French Embassy, my husband and I arrived at the lower entrance of the building, were each greeted by our assigned escorts, and then we all ascended a winding staircase to the dining room. I was seated next to my charming French escort in the center of the long table. My husband escorted his lady to a seat across from me.

"Where you sat in relation to the host and hostess (one at each end of the table) was an indication of your rank. The salt and pepper were the key. About a quarter of the way down the table from each end were the salt and pepper shakers. If you were seated *above the salt*, you were nearer the host or hostess, an indication of your higher status. If you were *below the salt*, your status was lower. We were in the middle of the table, as far below the salt as we could have been! Just as the soup was served I was approached by one of the waiters who told me 'Master Stephen would like to speak with you...on the telephone.' I had to catch the eye of my hostess, Madame Bonne, the wife of the ambassador, asked to be excused, and make my way from room to room until I finally found the library. My son (Master Stephen) said, "Mom, whose turn is it to have TV, Carol's or mine?" At that moment, there was no question: I was definitely *below the salt!*"

"One of the benefits of living in our nation's capital is meeting people from other countries. I find it fascinating to learn about other ways of doing things and other cultures. And, of course, the people are the very finest. After three years of living in our nation's capital and meeting so many interesting people from other cultures, I discovered they almost all had one thing in common. When they were nearing the end of the tour of service, I would ask them, 'Are you happy to be going back home?' They would answer both yes and no. Invariably they felt they hadn't had the opportunity to really get to know Americans personally. They hadn't really made friends. In a diplomatic and political setting, that is difficult to do The events attended in Washington are usually large and impersonal, maybe once or twice a year, and there is little, if any, opportunity to get to know people personally. That is the norm. It seemed to me that what was needed was the reverse.

"This inspired me to start a club. It would have limited membership to keep it small, no more than 20 members, and would have only four rules: No Politics, No Publicity, No Projects and No Protocol! The purpose would be to make personal friendships without getting tripped up by rules and protocol. We would be on a first-name basis, meet on common ground with no political agenda and learn to know each other as people, in relaxed relationships. Not only would it help Internationals make the friends they hoped for, it would make Washington a little more like home, and a lot more human. I put a committee together to help me get the club organized and we had our first meeting of the International Club I in 1953."

Marian and her committee invited 20 women to be the first members: 10 wives of the men serving in the diplomatic corps from all different countries, 6 wives of the men who served on the House Foreign Affairs Committee (3 Republican and 3 Democrat) and 4 wives of the men who served on The Senate Foreign Relations Committee (2 Republican and 2 Democrat). They called each other by their first names and they never had to think about where the salt shaker was! It all worked successfully, and 46 years later, it's still working beautifully.

Marian went on to start six clubs in five years, the first three for wives of congressmen and diplomats, and the last three clubs for wives of congressmen, diplomats, cabinet members, military top brass and the supreme court. Since the first clubs all had limited membership, in 1959, she started the Welcome to Washington International Club with open membership — any International and any American could join. This club has 850 members spread over 69 countries of the world! This one charter club has spawned to 13 other Welcome Clubs. Thanks to Marian, and those she has inspired, there are now International Clubs and Welcome Clubs in, England, Belgium, Germany, Denver (Colorado),

Florida, Switzerland, Madagascar, South Africa, and New Delhi, India.

While Ross Adair was helping manage the nation's business in the House of Representatives, Marian was managing to make people feel at home and make new friends in Washington. She started six clubs in five years, then ten years later, did three more International Clubs. Modestly, she says, "I didn't do this by myself, you know! I had a great deal of help and the other committee members deserve most of the credit. I don't. I feel honored and privileged to have friends all over the world as a result of that first club meeting. This has changed my entire life."

Conservatively speaking, the clubs have changed and enriched the lives of many thousands of women, all over the world. Many have said joining the club was the best thing they had done. It opened doors for them, and introduced them to people they would not have met otherwise. Friendships formed in the clubs have been cemented into friendships that are still ongoing.

In 1970 Ross Adair was defeated in his race for re-election. He had been the Minority Chairman of the Foreign Affairs Committee in the House. Then President Nixon recognized Ross' ability with foreign affairs, and appointed him Ambassador to Ethiopia. From 1971 to 1974, Marian and Ross served their country well on the foreign field, continuing the goodwill ambassadorship they started in Washington, and promoting international friendships everywhere they went.

"When you arrive in Washington, it's very hard to break into the social and political structure," explains Marian. You usually hang around with your political friends. To break out of the mold, you need some type of entree: the clubs are the entree. I started them to help people get to know each other and enjoy Washington. My husband and I always focused on our constituents, our faith, and our international friends. We were determined to get acquainted with people. This was a way of making it easier for others to do the same, especially those from foreign countries who were serving here. These clubs are not your normal block party. But then, Washington is not your normal city."

When a dynamic woman who has spent her life beside her husband serving others is widowed, her life can either expand, or contract. It cannot ever again be quite the same as it was. Which direction life takes is a decision each new widow must make for herself. Marian chose continued expansion. She explains, "I didn't know where to make my home after Ross died. I had a home in Fort Wayne, and one in Washington. The first year I spent time in both. Then one day I realized that the action is in Washington! So this is where I am, too!"

Marian Adair has had a world of influence on women whose husbands are in government service, both here and abroad. She is quick to mention she feels privileged to have been instrumental in furthering global understanding. "Each of us has talents," she says. We all have at least one! I believe we should use our talents to help others in whatever way we can. It doesn't have to be a major accomplishment. It can be a minor thing, such as making a phone call, or making cookies for someone, or sending a letter to encourage someone who's down. We should share our God-given talents, because that's why we're here — to be of service."

Anna Gould

Spreading Sunshine to Families with Seriously Ill Children

Pat answers are not part of the program at Camp Sunshine in Casco, Maine. Instead, there's plenty of family fun and support for families with a seriously ill child. Anna Gould and her husband, Larry, make sure of that. Larry was CEO of a large corporation in Boston and had purchased the prime resort location now called Point Sebago. Anna took over the marketing of Point Sebago and has been overseeing the daily operations and planing its growth ever since. "I've always enjoyed working with people," she smiles. "I wouldn't be happy sitting in a cubicle with just machines."

While spinning the TV dial one day, they caught a segment about a camp in Georgia for children with terminal illnesses. The story touched both Anna and Larry very deeply. The idea for a similar camp at Point Sebago was born. They did some research and made contact with the people at Dana-Farber in Boston, a hospital specializing in childhood leukemia. The head of pediatric oncology suggested they *not* start a children's camp. He pointed out that the real need was for the entire family to have a break, not just the sick children. "Actually, that was a whole lot easier for us to handle," Anna explains. "We had families at Point Sebago all the time. I had been wondering how I was going to get enough counselors to take care of just the kids and what to do about

73

supervision. Taking care of the whole family is what we were doing anyway. It was a natural."

Camp Sunshine opened the following spring in 1984. Forty families of children with cancer enjoyed a marvelous week at beautiful Sebago Lake, courtesy of the Goulds. That's right. There's no charge to the families. Now, for two weeks in June and two weeks in September, the Goulds do not accept paying guests. The entire facility is turned over to the families of children with serious illnesses, free of charge. They call it Camp Sunshine.

Why would a popular resort give up the opportunity to produce income during their prime season? "I'm a mother and a grandmother," Anna explains. "I know how helpless you feel when your child is sick. I can't imagine how devastating it must be when your child has a terminal illness. When all the money and all the medical technology in the world is useless against a disease that is killing your child, it has to be the most agonizing kind of frustration. We have this beautiful facility and we saw a way we could help a little bit. So we extend hospitality to entire families who are in these situations. We've been very fortunate, and this is our way of giving something back."

The Goulds were totally overwhelmed with the response. "We felt that we did so little – just made our facilities available – and it meant so much to the families who came!" The camp program is basically the same that Point Sebago offers to regular campers. There is a structured program broken into age groups with activities that are age-appropriate. There are parents' groups, including discussion groups with a psychologist as the facilitator.

"As much as you think you understand because you're a parent," Anna says, "It's very difficult to comprehend the enormity of the day to day issues these families have to go through when a child has a serious illness. The focus of the entire family's life becomes the sick child. The other children sometimes feel left out or neglected, even if they aren't. The parents don't go out to dinner anymore. Often one parent assumes the financial support of the family while the other one takes on the additional daily care required. Life is planned around doctor appointments and hospital visits. Nothing is normal. When a child is sick for a week or two, that's one thing. But what do you do when it's 365 days a year for several years? That's an enormous amount of stress and many marriages don't survive. You have no alternative because the child has a life-threatening disease and life cannot be normal. The stress load is often more than the parents can bear."

Blessed with a healthy family, Anna admits she has no idea what it's like to have a terminally ill child. "All the trite sayings and pat answers in the world do nothing to help. The best thing to say is simply 'I'm sorry for what you're going through. How can I help?' The worst thing you can do is say, 'I know how you feel.' Unless your own child has had the same illness, you *don't* know how they feel or what they're going through."

Families spend a week with other families who are dealing with the same illness. Over the past fourteen years, there have been weeks dedicated to families of kids with cancer, kidney disease, cystic fibrosis, fanconi anemia, hemophilia, diabetes and other life-threatening diseases. And they come from all over the world. "We group the families this way because we find they have more in common with other families suffering through the same illness and they can better help each other and share information," Anna explains. "Because I want to understand, I sit in on the parent sessions, even though my children are healthy."

In the morning, everyone has breakfast together. Then they can choose to go to their respective age group meetings or spend time with their families. They're not restricted or forced to attend any meetings. They can participate or not.

One of the volunteers, Joe Pappalardo, took it upon himself to build up a cadre of volunteers, and they come back week after week, year after year. It restores your faith in humanity when you see something like this happening. "Our volunteers are exceptional," smiles Anna. "They give not only their time, but their emotional support. They literally adopt a Camp Sunshine family for a week. Many of them keep in touch after their stay at camp is over, developing friendships that go on for years. We need all types of volunteers – from babysitters to counselors to dishwashers to arts and crafts directors and meal servers. We assign one volunteer per family, unless there is a child who needs a volunteer assigned just to him or her because of special needs. When you volunteer, you are expected to be there for the whole week. Local people do go home to sleep, but they're back in the morning. Even when they're not on duty, they still stay. They give about eight days' work in the five days they're here and they really make a difference. We have a pediatrician and psychologist and professional help for each week of camp. The program is designed to focus on the specific issues the parents, the patients, and the healthy siblings face, in order to give all family members additional strength and perspective in facing the struggles brought on by a severe illness. Everything we can do to provide a happy, nearly care-free vacation for the family is carefully thought out and taken care of. The letters we get back from people tell us how much these volunteers give of themselves and how much it means to the families who come. We couldn't do it without them."

One family expressed their thanks this way:

Being at Camp Sunshine was the most positive thing that happened to our family this year. We met wonderful people with whom we could share common experiences, people who could truly understand, because they were undergoing a challenge in their lives, too. Thank you for giving our family the opportunity to enjoy a truly wonderful, sharing, and loving, experience. Another family said: *Camp Sunshine was our first respite from home, reality, and cancer care. It was an experience that gave something to us – it didn't take. Camp Sunshine and its 'Angels of Mercy' gave us back our sanity.*

The Goulds donate not only the entire facility, but the services of their staff as well when camp is in session. The food alone to feed 50 families and 80 volunteers for a week requires a sizeable amount of money, so Anna and Larry set up a public nonprofit corporation to handle donations.

What has all this done for Anna Gould? "Being a part of Camp Sunshine has given me a different perspective on humanity. I now have a lot less tolerance for problems that people perceive as devastating. A minor altercation with a spouse or a child is not life-threatening, but some people let that totally consume them. When I see what some families endure – the heartache, the financial burdens, the helplessness to 'make it go away' for their children, and the quiet, brave suffering of the children – I have little patience with minuscule everyday problems that can be easily resolved. Working with Camp Sunshine has given me a proper perspective on what is really important. What I've learned is to put my priorities in order. What really counts is family."

Anna feels that the little things are very important. If a family has an infant, a volunteer babysitter is assigned to take care of that infant so the rest of the family can be free of that responsibility. One night during a family's stay, there is a *parents only* dinner. For most, it's the first time a husband and wife had had dinner alone since the child's illness was diagnosed. "The infrastructure of the family has been broken down due to the demands of the illness of one child. Some relatives simply cannot deal with the impending tragedy, or with the day to day living with it, so they withdraw from the family in an attempt to give some semblance of normalcy to life. Of course, this only adds to the pain and suffering. Total strangers reach out with love and compassion and help heal the peripheral hurts caused by the situation. By the end of the week, it's the volunteers who feel lucky to be involved."

Anna talks about the transformation that takes in the families. "It's difficult to describe the level of gratification you get from seeing children come in with a morose, downcast demeanor and in a couple of days they're acting like a normal kid, running around playing. When a child is bald due to chemotherapy treatments, the other children there are bald, too, so no one feels out of place. Everyone here is in the same boat. And for the parents, it may be the first time in years they've been relaxed enough and free enough to walk down the beach hand in hand. Or dance together. Or had time to catch their breath. Where else can they go as a family and not worry about the cost of a week's vacation at a resort?"

There is a medical doctor on site at all times, and the child's medical records are part of the application process. In fact, the children are referred by their hospitals and doctors. Then the selection process begins. Over 1700 families have spent a week at Camp Sunshine, but it's not easy to decide who will or will not be accepted. There is never enough room to take everyone who wants to come.

Realizing that a permanent, year-round home was needed for the camp, Anna and her husband have donated 15 acres adjacent to Sebago Lake. All necessary local and state approvals have been obtained. In the summer of 1992, The Maine National Guard selected Camp Sunshine as a project and brought in their heavy equipment to clear the land in accordance with the master plan. "It looked like a scene out of M.A.S.H.!"

laughs Anna. "It was really great to watch." Many local businesses have helped. But more help is needed.

The week-long program will be offered from April through November and would accommodate over 1800 families. When she talks about the future, Anna gets a sparkle in her eyes. "There are a lot of camps for sick children. But we don't know of any for their entire family."

All that is needed now is $4 million to finish building the permanent facility. It will be a wonderful place of healing and happiness for families struggling with the enormous impact of tragic childhood illness and the accompanying disruption of family, social and economic life. The new facility is now under construction and will include a Family Activity Center with a dining room for 275 people, a large activity pavilion, a teen center, an adult conference center, an arts and crafts center, a nursery and tot center, an indoor swimming pool, a clinic and administrative offices. A Family Living Center with 40 suites for up to six people each, and a Volunteer Living Center for up to 60 volunteers are also included in the plan. There is already an administration building, a large gazebo and restroom with access to the beach and Sebago Lake. This was built with donated funds and most of the lumber was donated by the local lumberyard, Hancock Lumber Company. It's beautiful!

In addition to all she does for Camp Sunshine, Anna is Director of Operations for Point Sebago, a three-season resort. A new 18-hole championship golf course is in full swing and was rated by Golf Digest as the 4th best new affordable course in North America in 1996. They are selling ownership sites around the golf course, complete with an 800 square foot resort cottage. Part of the proceeds from the sale of these ownership sites will go to expand Camp Sunshine. (Why isn't that a surprise?)

Needless to say, Anna's employees admire and respect her. "She's very fair," said one. "It's a great place to work." It's quiet and peaceful at Point Sebago, even with 2500 to 3000 people enjoying the facilities. There's a sense of community here, even when it's not Camp Sunshine week. The local high school uses Point Sebago's tennis courts in the spring, compliments of the Goulds. It's definitely a family environment, all year long.

"I think the family structure is very important to anyone's stability," says Anna. "Someone has to help these families in crisis. We do what we can by providing this place."

One Summer of Sunshine

A boy running here
A girl playing there
There seem to be children everywhere

Some shout with joy, some scream with delight
Some cuddle a toy and some dream of flight

We look at them now, so ill yet so brave
How cruel this world – it's their life that we crave

What lies ahead? What future is there?
Their life is so fleeting, today seems so bare

It doesn't seem fair – why them and why now?
How can they endure – God, please tell me how?

We pray and we weep, yet outwardly smile
Our hearts ache, and we still hope for a while

Yet we know deep inside, that in life there is hope
And we look to the SUNSHINE – it helps us to cope

One day at a time is all that we ask
With hope for tomorrow, so easy a task

Just one more day, one of fun, free of pain
And then still another, it can't be in vain

Hope, joy and laughter – we need them all three
And at CAMP SUNSHINE we get them for free

We simply can't know what tomorrow will bring
Today is what counts – just hear us sing!

A boy running here
A girl playing there
We're so happy to see children everywhere!

Colene Daniel

Finding Diamonds in the Rough in Baltimore's Inner City Kids

"It doesn't matter how you're raised or how little you have, your success in life is determined by how you use what you have." Colene Daniel speaks from personal experience. Colene is Vice-President of Corporate and Community Services for the Johns Hopkins Health System in Baltimore, Maryland. Against overwhelming odds, she has risen to the top of her profession by sheer determination, academic achievement, and a lot of help from people who believed in her.

When Colene was eight years old and living in an impoverished ghetto of Cincinnati, Ohio, with her mother and four brothers and sisters, her life was torn apart.

"We were living in a sub-basement apartment with only two rooms," she remembers. "We weren't the poorest family in the neighborhood, even though our bathtub was a washtub we filled with boiled water to bathe. One night we were asleep when there was a terrible banging on our door. Outside the window we could see flashing lights from several police cars. The five of us were taken from our beds; for the next six years we were separated. I was taken to a temporary holding house for foster children and held there for about six months. No one told me why we had been taken from our mother and sent to separate foster homes. I went from being a kid who had never known any trouble to being with kids who were tough criminals. I quickly learned to hate the world.

"My first foster home gave up on me after six months. I was then sent to a place called *The Colored Orphanage of Cincinnati* which housed around a hundred children, where I lived for four years. The building had been a very large hospital, with very large grounds. We were told there were ghosts in the attic, left over from people who had died there when it was a hospital, and we believed them. Many of the supervisors were not educated or trained to handle children who were unhappy due to their displacement, and their frustration would lead to very harsh punishments. One night, several children began to have a pillow fight. The supervisor told us to stop, but we were just having too much fun. The supervisor punished us by taking us to the attic and locking each of us in separate closets. All night long in the darkness, I heard the screams of fear and the sounds of my friends scratching at the doors trying to get out. I thought if a spirit were coming to get me, I wanted it to be a *good* spirit, so I prayed all night. The experience had lasting effects on us: a few did not speak for several days; two became very bitter and angry with society; one at age sixteen committed suicide; yet *my* faith became stronger. I believe that God saved me for a reason, and on that night I decided I would always take control of my own life.

"The only explanation I ever got for why we had been taken from our home was that one of my relatives had wanted my little brother and had complained that my mother was unfit to raise us. When I was twelve, the orphanage was demolished, and I was sent to one foster home for about a year, and then to another foster home. I was told repeatedly that I had little worth, I was not very bright, and that I would never amount to anything in life. My only escape came from working in the kitchen. Because of my poor self-image, I had few friends, so I sought comfort in food and books. During the day my schoolmates laughed at me, and at night in the foster homes I lived with abuse.

"At age fifteen, I decided it was time to be on my own. I tried to live with my mother, but we had grown too far apart. After a couple of months, I rented a basement apartment at $54 per month. I worked after school and weekends, got myself into one of Cincinnati's best public high schools, and used a false ID to receive food stamps. I had never done well on standardized tests, so I was placed in the slower classes. However, my teachers found out that I read Shakespeare and Homer for enjoyment, so they went to the administration and moved me into regular classes. Within a year, I was taking advanced courses for literature and history.

"Being moved to different foster homes and being shuttled from school to school, had caused me to fall behind academically, so I had to make up six years of education in three years! By my senior year in high school, I was in the honor society, involved in the student achievement program and in student government, and holding down three part-time jobs. My principal and teachers had never seen my parents and began raising questions about my parental guidance. So I recruited two alcoholics from my neighborhood, coached them, and introduced them at a school function as my parents. No one said anything afterward, so I thought I was home free. My relief was short-lived: my principal told me my secret was out and I had to go to court because I was under 18. I argued that I paid all my bills, stayed out of trouble and there was no way I would go back to a foster home at this point in my life! Two of my teachers agreed to be my guardians; I was living on my own, but under their supervision, I was allowed to complete my education.

"I had been attending the Upward Bound program which prepared minority students for college. My scores on the standardized tests weren't good enough for a private college, so I attended the University of Cincinnati. I wrote a letter to the dean, explaining what I'd been through and how far I'd come, promising if they would give me a chance, I would show them I could make it through college. Again, God answered my prayers, and the Assistant Dean told me, 'If you have that much determination in you, you will succeed in college.' She had to initial my college application papers, accepting responsibility for me, because my mother had refused to sign them. As with my high school English teachers, someone believed in me and wanted to help me. I graduated with a Bachelor of Science degree in Speech Pathology and Audiology and was listed in *Who's Who in American Universities*. I realized that even though I might never score high on standardized tests, I had a tremendous capacity to learn and the determination to succeed."

While working as a speech pathologist in Houston, Texas, Colene discovered that she had a natural talent in administration. "I took the entrance examination for graduate school and I scored very low on the

Graduate Record Exams, so I wrote a letter to Texas Woman's University asking to be admitted on a provisional status." Once again, someone gave her a chance, and her application was provisionally approved. Two years later she graduated with a Masters in Health Care Administration.

After graduation, Colene completed her residency and began working as an administrator. She advanced up the corporate ladder while working in Saudi Arabia, China, Kenya, Houston and Chicago for government, and for both profit and nonprofit hospitals. In 1991, Colene was hired as Vice President of Corporate Services at The Johns Hopkins Hospital in Baltimore. During the first two years she began to identify two aspects of Hopkins. The clinical staff had a strong desire not only to treat disease but to also *prevent* disease. The service employees desired to have a better understanding of how clinical research was being conducted to allay fears of abuse and wanted more participation in selecting programs that were being planned to benefit the community around the hospital. Both groups had similar goals, but were not aware of what the other group was doing.

The CEO saw the need to synthesize the two groups and formed the Department of Community Services, with Colene at the helm. However, community services and community health were new disciplines to learn while implementing the new vision: to revitalize the East Baltimore community. Since Colene had little experience in public health, she applied to Johns Hopkins School of Hygiene and Public Health. As in the past, the registrar was concerned about her low Graduate Record Exam scores. Colene was asked to take 16 hours of course work on a probationary basis to see if she would qualify for the program. In spite of her intensive 80-hour hospital schedule, she completed the 16 hours with an A average. Three years later she earned her second Masters. "I have *two* Masters degrees, and if you asked me to take a standardized test today, I *still* would not come close to an acceptable score!"

Colene Daniel is achieving her dream. "I have about twenty more years of goals to accomplish in terms of achieving professional and educational advancement," she smiles. As a much-respected health care administrator and one of the leading African-Americans in health care, she could now rest on her hard-earned laurels. But she doesn't. The Board of Trustees at Johns Hopkins has committed to the revitalization of East Baltimore and this commitment has provided opportunity for staff

84

to work hand-in-hand with East Baltimore residents. To that end, Colene has worked to improve Corporate Services of the hospital. "Many of our service workers are from East Baltimore, and it is important for our hospital support services to be as good as our clinical care and research. As Corporate Services continues to improve its delivery, the service staff experiences the importance of their contribution to the Hospital.

Colene also spends her days focusing Johns Hopkins Community Services on remedying problems in the community. "In order for academic centers to be successful over the long-term, we must become interested in the total community. We are involved in housing, economic development, youth services, public safety, community health and sanitation and education." Colene addresses community needs on several different levels; the policy level requires her participation on community-based boards, the management level requires her to plan and implement projects, and the interactive level is where she personally provides service. "I can honestly say I love joining with community residents to obtain new Block Grants to renovate 700 homes, remove lead paint, provide adequate heating, rezone city streets to reduce violent crime and work in partnerships with local businesses to improve economic development in East Baltimore. Each project reduces a potential health problem."

Colene Daniel has used the obstacles thrown in her path as stepping stones to personal and professional achievement. She uses these achievements to inspire inner-city children to stay in school and to mentor college students. Her immense energy and dedication has led to recognition by her peers as a top-notch communicator, leader, and executive. Colene has recently been appointed to the new Baltimore City School Board of Commissioners to improve public education.

"Education is second in importance to good health, and the next most important resource a child needs to make it, no matter what their race or economic status. When I talk to children and discover they have lost hope, I tell them the hardships can be overcome with hope, determination, and education. When I speak with adults, asking them to take a risk and give our youth, particularly our troubled youth, a chance, I tell them what it meant to me as a young girl to be given a chance. No matter how bad the situation became, how cold, hungry, or alone I felt, I was always given a chance to receive a good education, mentoring from

85

teachers and others, and hope from church and God. Today's inner-city children will be some of tomorrow's leaders. We must seek out these *diamonds in the rough*."

Jude Hannemann

Reaching Out to Cancer Patients Is Her Way of Life

There's a palpable energy that floats around Jude Hannemann. And then the quiet aura of inner grace supersedes it. Here is a woman who knows suffering first hand, and has triumphed over it by helping others who are struggling with a diagnosis of cancer. Jude has never had cancer herself, although once there was a devastating threat that proved false. "I don't know why that happened to me," she muses, "except that it did give me some sense of the emotional turmoil people endure once the threat of cancer is there. Now when I counsel cancer patients, I understand what's happening to them as I never understood before. It's added new depths to my compassion and sympathy."

Jude and her husband, Jake (chief of radiation therapy at Maine Medical Center), spend three weekends a year – and many hours in between – hosting *Discovery Weekend*, a program conceived in 1980 by Dr. Ronald Carroll, a Portland oncologist. Dr. Carroll invited the Hannemanns to help him develop and manage the program which addresses the needs of both the people who have been diagnosed with cancer *and* their caregivers. Drs. Carroll and Hannemann worked together in the oncology unit of the hospital and were acutely aware of the degree of suffering involved with a cancer diagnosis. Jude was (and still is) a professor at the university, a homemaker, and a mother, and was not that involved with her husband's work. She knew in her head what a cancer diagnosis must do to a person emotionally as well as physically, but she had no idea of the depth of suffering endured by someone in that position.

"Suffering, as I have come to understand it," Jude explains, "is more than the physical pain. The word cancer brings two things to mind: pain, and death. I now know that some of the deepest suffering the patients experience is the threat to the integrity of the person – to what holds the person together and what holds his or her life together. It's a much deeper threat than just physical. It's the disintegration of their identities: the physical incapacity that robs them of the ability to work and provide for themselves and their families, the inability to perform the simple tasks of living – cooking dinner, shopping for groceries, mowing the lawn or clearing the snow from the driveway. Deep, demoralizing, defeating questions begin to chip away at whatever emotional stability is left: What have I done with my life? What is left? Is there anything worth fighting for in life? Is there anything after this life? What's going to happen next?"

Jude and the other staff volunteers at Discovery Weekend help cancer patients gain a fresh perspective, not only on their disease, but also on life after the diagnosis. They explore communication skills, medical information, personal coping skills and spirituality. The meals are good, the jazz band on Saturday night has everyone dancing or at least tapping their feet, and friendships are made and renewed. There are serious moments, as well might be expected. One of the sessions splits the patients from their caregivers so both groups feel free to express things they normally don't voice. For many, it's the first time the caregivers have the opportunity to let down their guard and express their grief and discouragement – something they would not allow themselves to do in front of the ones they're caring for.

"The patients discover there is a full life, love and laughter after a diagnosis of cancer. And their loved ones who are the caregivers discover the strength of mutual support. The thing we work at the hardest is giving them a sense of hope, that life is still worth living, there are still things to laugh about, and that life can be lived to its fullest regardless of the circumstances of the cancer. Life is still to be cherished, preserved and shared.

"We laugh a lot at Discovery Weekend," Jude smiles. "I remember the time a speaker arrived at the conference center to give a presentation. He asked at the desk where the cancer group was meeting and was directed down the hall. Hearing riotous laughter coming from the room he was told to go to, he walked right by it, and found himself at the end of the hall. He returned to the desk, certain he had been given the wrong directions."

When the Weekends began, Jude and the other volunteers wondered if their program were adequate. Driving between enormous snowbanks to the conference center for the first Weekend, Jude and Jake wondered what it would be like to live for 48 hours with people who were facing such suffering. They had gathered a group of patients, clergy, a psychologist, a psychiatrist, two physicians and a volunteer nurse. They needn't have worried. The patients themselves made it easier, by opening up and being willing to be vulnerable publicly. One by one they shared their fears, their triumphs, their hopes. They broke down and wept. They hugged and supported each other. The outcome was certain knowledge that Discovery Weekends were here to stay – an integral part of therapy.

Since then, different features and experiences have been added to the agenda, but there is always a panel where patients share their experiences and discuss their own adjustments, failures and successes, pain and joy. Not all patients are willing to air their despair or share their emotional upheavals with everyone. But when they do, they find it cathartic. "It takes a lot of inner strength to sit in front of everyone else and tell your deepest feelings, but it really does help others who may be struggling with the very same thoughts," Jude says. "Some patients just listen. Other feel comfortable telling it all. It depends on where they are in their treatment and on their individual inner strength." All the activities at Discovery Weekend are optional and each patient decides the level of his or her own participation.

Unexpectedly, Jude has developed wonderful friendships with some of the patients. One of the first was a woman of twenty-five who had cancer of the mumps gland. Half of her face was paralyzed and the other half was normal. She had exceptional inner beauty and courage. Since the woman's husband was often at sea, Jude offered to take her for her treatments, and often took her home to be with her own family. The Hannemann boys grew up knowing that reaching out to others is a way of life, not just something you do once in a while when you're feeling magnanimous. Discovery Weekends and the resulting friendships are a part of the Hannemann's family life.

The Discovery Weekend program is a project of The Maine Cancer Research and Education Foundation (MCREF). The Foundation has made it possible for those who cannot afford the modest lodging fee to attend the Weekends. Attending one of the Weekends makes a tremendous difference in people's lives.

"I'm a devout coward," Jude laughs. "When we first started the Discovery Weekend project, I felt I wouldn't be very helpful. When my children had upset stomachs, mine was upset, too! When I see other people cry, I cry. When I see someone faint, I faint. I thought I would just be a part of the problem, not the solution. But I was wrong. When I saw the courage of the cancer patients, I gained courage. When they described their struggles, I remembered my own struggles and I was able to relate to them. Their faith and hope boosted my own faith and hope. My life has been enriched beyond measure because of the people I've met at the Weekends. Before I got involved in this project, many of the relationships in my life were of a social nature and somewhat superficial. But I found out it's impossible to relate superficially with people struggling on such deep levels. This has been an adventure in personal relationships for me. The cancer patients and their families have opened their hearts and their homes to me. They have been my teachers; I have been the student. They have taught me the definition of courage and the resiliency of the human spirit. They have been friends of astonishing support through the difficult times in my own life. Their suffering has qualified them to love. And I have been the blessed recipient of that love."

Jude draws heavily on her Christian faith for inner strength and grace in everyday life. One of the goals of Discovery Weekend is that every cancer patient attending would be encouraged to progress on his or her spiritual journey, whatever form or level it implies. Over 2,000 people have attended Discovery Weekend since the program began eighteen years ago. Not all of them survived the duel with cancer. But their lives were all made a little easier by sharing support with others who were also struggling with the disease. Having seen for herself how much the program helps people cope and how much their lives have been enriched by just being there, Jude would like to see other Discovery Weekend programs in other states.

"My involvement with Discovery Weekends has been a source of personal enrichment for me," she reflects. "It's true that when you reach out to others, you get back much more than you give. The more you give, the more you get back. It's a wonderful unending cycle!"

Anita Martinez

Using Performing Arts to Give Hispanic Children Cultural Pride

Brilliant colors, flying feet and a healthy Latin beat are what Anita Nanez Martinez has used to bring pride to the hearts and smiles to the faces of Hispanic children in Dallas, Texas. Anita's flamboyant *Ballet Folklorico* dance company raises the level of cultural pride while teaching self esteem and confidence. "I started this dance company twenty-three years ago," she explains, "because I came from an Hispanic background, too, and I wanted the children to be able to hold up their heads with pride in their cultural heritage and traditions. At that time, the most heavily Hispanic area of Dallas was the weak link in our city.

"The largest percentage of school age children came from that district, yet 72% of the people there lived at poverty level or below. There were few gutters, few streetlights and very little indoor plumbing. It was a difficult place to foster pride in anything. If we wanted Dallas to be known as a great city, we needed to fix this situation."

Because Anita was serving in many civic organizations at the time, her house was full of projects she was involved in. "I had work spread out on every surface available," she laughs. "One night an Hispanic woman called me and suggested I run for the Dallas City Council. At first I thought it was just a nice compliment that she would think of me, but as

93

I listened to her, and looked around at all the piles of projects, I realized I'd be more effective in what I was trying to accomplish if I were on the Council. After much discussion with my family, I tossed my sombrero into the political arena, vowing to give the race everything I had."

In 1969, Anita Nanez Martinez became the first Hispanic woman in the United States to be elected to a city council. According to the Dallas Herald, her victory was slightly short of miraculous. Twenty-eight people had been running for only 11 positions on the council and Anita was running for the most heavily contested seat of all. "I had been very involved in the community, and people knew me. As soon as I announced my candidacy, my phone started ringing off the hook. I put everyone to work, even the children! Everyone helped get the vote out, and it worked. I promised to use my position on the council to get the needs of the people addressed."

Anita had known that pride in their cultural heritage and traditions was very lacking in the young Hispanic children of Dallas. Throughout both of her consecutive terms as councilwoman at large (1969-1973) she fought with integrity to raise the standard of living in the Hispanic district. That was also the period of time when both a beautiful new city hall (designed by I.M. Pei) and the Dallas-Fort Worth airport were being built. Keeping her promise to the people, Anita challenged the council to bring the long-neglected, dismally poor Hispanic area of Dallas up to the standards of the rest of the city. "This area was located directly across the river from the central business district," she explains. "I met with the people and asked them to write down ten things they felt they needed in their neighborhood. They wanted what everyone else in the city already had: a free-standing library, swimming pool, paved streets, a health clinic, a recreation center...normal city services." Anita took the wish list and went to work, convincing the council to pour over $8 million into the area. Modestly she says, "We were very effective in addressing the needs."

A long-awaited, desperately-needed recreational center was built in 1975 in the same area of Dallas. The building was named after Anita, in recognition of her work with the youth and the leadership she had given to the blue collar grassroots people in the poorest area of Dallas. By 1985, this was the most heavily used of the 48 recreational centers in the city, even though it was the smallest in size. It was obvious that an expansion plan was needed. A second story was added, as well as a state of the art kitchen, a computer area and a spring-loaded dance floor. It went from 14,000 to 38,000 square feet on the 1985 Dallas Municipal Bond Program. "It's a showplace now," Anita smiles. "But one of the best things we have going for us is the spirit of volunteer service. Everyone pitches in. We don't have just Hispanic pride here now, we have family pride!"

"I was the fifth of six children raised in a moderate home in the Little Mexico area of Dallas where there was a large pocket of Hispanics," Anita remembers. "My parents couldn't afford dance lessons, but a woman in our neighborhood took an interest in us and taught us the dance steps, and her mother made our costumes out of crepe paper so we could produce shows for our neighbors. When people applauded, it boosted my confidence and made me feel good about myself. I reasoned that a similar experience would do the same for other Hispanic children. The saddest discrimination is the one you bring on yourself, for lack of confidence in who you are as a person. Through this art form they could relate to the music and to the dance so they would feel they were contributors to society."

When the center opened in 1975, Anita had already retired from the council. Realizing the best hope for the city was in its children, Anita founded her dance company: Ballet Folklorico. "This was the anchor in my plan to instill personal and cultural pride in the Hispanic children. I reasoned that whether they spectated or participated, they would still hear the music and learn about their cultural heritage." The first classes were held in the gym, and the program was so successful, the city asked the dance company to perform all over the city. Then came the landmark decision from the city council to allocate funds for a part-time instructor to teach folklorico. (Folklorico is the folk lore of any culture. Hispanic folklore is made up of Spanish, Mexican, Indian, Russian, and German folklore.)

The Ballet Folklorico program brings families together. Parents get involved with the children and see their kids in a new light. They see them being applauded, so the child goes back to a more supportive environment. Parents volunteer at the center, by sewing costumes, selling tickets – whatever needs to be done. "We give a lot of scholarships because people can't afford classes," Anita admits. "They pay us back by working in the center and helping with the program, so they have a stake in its success. When you give people something, they'll take it, but unless they give something in return, you take away their dignity. That's what it's all about: giving people dignity and pride in who they are.

"Being a student of Ballet Folklorico teaches children confidence-building blocks. They learn how to take responsibility, how to see a task through to completion, and how to be a team player. They become well-rounded individuals, with a healthy self esteem. This is the most powerful form of art, because your body is the instrument. Obviously, the children in the program don't all become professional dancers! These lessons can be applied to any career they choose. School teachers have told us that they can tell which children came from our program, because they are more respectful and are real team players.

"Ballet Folklorico is a history lesson learned through music and expressed through movement — dance. All people can contribute their uniqueness for the enhancement of the whole. Texas history has had the flags of 6 nations flown over its soil. No single group can take full credit for what is Texas, or what is America. Our dancers are ambassadors, bringing together all people in the spirit of cooperation, with a mission to enlighten everyone about a culture that is older than either Egypt, China or Rome."

In 1994, Anita received an award from the Dallas Historical Society for excellence in arts leadership. She sums up her vision this way: "If you have children, the most important thing you can do for them is to give them your time, your talents and your treasure. Do that first. Then your efforts will be multiplied through them to help the total community. There is no quick easy fix to mold and develop a child. It takes a lot of time.

Teach your children the value of communication and teamwork. We must teach all of our children that good citizenship is a balanced view of every individual's contribution, not just their own."

Susan Stanford-Rue

Helping Women Find Healing and Forgiveness for Pregnancy Loss

Susan Stanford-Rue had it all: husband, promising career, beautiful home in the country, and a wonderful horse named Morning Mist who was a true soul-mate. And then she lost it all. But it was after she lost it all that she eventually found real happiness. And it was because she was willing to share her story that hundreds of women have found healing and forgiveness for pregnancy loss due to either miscarriage or abortion.

At college Susan fell head-over-heels in love with a man who offered her unbounded love, and they planned to marry. Then, through a casual phone conversation with a mutual friend, Susan learned that her fiancé had been married and divorced — facts he had withheld from her. She was devastated. According to the teachings of her church, she could not marry him without the first marriage being annulled. After confrontation, separation, and heart-wrenching emotional pain, she put the marriage and relationship on hold, waiting for Frank (not his real name) to work things out. Four long years later, the annulment came through and they were married. That should have been the happy ending, but it was just the beginning of the turmoil ahead.

They bought a wonderful house in the country, complete with

97

stables, and Frank began to travel more for his career in investments. Susan enrolled in a doctorate program in counseling. In addition to working part-time, studying full-time, she found herself alone more often than not, with the full responsibility for running the house, taking care of their boarded horses, and trying to live up to her idea of being a good wife. Frank became more and more remote, never showing any interest in helping her with all she was dealing with, and disinterested in her doctoral studies. Their relationship spiraled downward, the stress spiraling upward.

The inequity of the situation hit her one night in the middle of a roaring blizzard in February. She had asked him to help her shovel out the two snowbound cars and move them into the garage and then help with the horses. As he settled into his favorite chair, his uncaring answer was, "What's for supper?" Furious, Susan bundled up and battled the storm alone for over two and a half hours. Stumbling back into the house, physically and emotionally drained, she saw Frank still sitting in his chair, reading. With tears streaming down her face as she changed out of her wet clothes and tried to get warm, she realized she no longer wanted to live the sham their marriage had become. The next morning, after Frank left for work, she packed a bag and moved to a friend's apartment. In the next few months she had to take exams and defend her doctoral thesis. She needed time away from the stress of the relationship. To keep her mind off the disaster at home, she spent as much time as possible studying with friends at school and finishing her thesis.

One friend in particular, Dan, also a doctoral student, offered Susan his support, and his love. The months of fighting with Frank had taken their toll. Dan was fun and attentive. They often studied together. Emotionally exhausted, she allowed Dan to comfort her, eagerly soaking up his attention and his love. "I still loved Frank and hoped to work out our marriage. I knew it was wrong to let myself get involved with Dan," she admits, "but I wasn't listening to my conscience." Dan was constantly there for her, supporting her in preparing for her doctoral thesis, comforting her and enjoying her company. That support became intimate and their physical involvement started. It was Dan who helped her celebrate passing her oral and written final exams. It was Dan who first called her Doctor Stanford. Frank hadn't called even once!

After a few months, Dan had an opportunity to go to the West Coast for the summer. Susan was actually relieved, thinking that with her studies completed and Dan out of the picture, she would now have the time to sort out her feelings and work out her relationship with Frank. "I was wrong," she says. "Time was the one thing I didn't have."

On the morning of her graduation, which should have been one of the happiest of her life, she winced as she put on her dress. For a couple of weeks there had been a tenderness in her breasts which she had been ignoring. There had been other signs she had been ignoring as well, such as refusing to count the number of days since her last period. The agonizing realization that she was pregnant hit her hard. The walk to commencement exercises was anything but joyful. When the president of the university handed her the coveted diploma and said, "Congratulations," she thought. Yeah, congratulations, Susan. You're pregnant. And the baby's father is not your husband.

The tug-of-war in Susan's conscience went on relentlessly. What was she going to do? How long had she been pregnant? "That was the worst part," she remembers. "I could not bring myself to think of the thing growing inside my body as a baby. Whenever the images began to form, I slammed the lid down on my thoughts and feelings. I don't know at exactly what point I decided this unwanted clump of tissue had to be removed from my body. I waffled every time I tried to pick up the phone to call a clinic and arrange the procedure. I couldn't even call it by its name: abortion. My Catholic upbringing rose and fell, rose and fell. The indecision unnerved me. But I had to do something because I was running out of time. I felt if I just got rid of the problem I would not have to think of this clump of cells as a baby. I picked up the phone and made the appointment. The sooner I do it, the sooner it will be behind me, I thought. I had no idea how naïve that thinking was.

The procedure itself was a pure hell of emotional and physical pain. Somehow, she got through it. But once it was over, and she began to feel better physically, her mind kicked into gear and the emotional torment began anew. "More than a baby had died in that room," I thought. "A part of me had died, too. Once I had had a personality, a life, a soul. Now I was a body with broken pieces inside. It was that sense of shattering that I could not get a grip on. I couldn't even cry. My grief, loss and shame had me in a prison. I was barely surviving.

"Unexpectedly, I got a call from Frank, asking me to stay at our house for a weekend to care for the horses while he was away on a trip. It was strange being back in the house, but good to see my horse, Morning Mist, again. Her company was a balm for my aching spirit. As I was preparing to leave on Sunday evening, Frank came home earlier than expected. We had a terrible argument, the pressure building to the bursting point. Frank kept bombarding me with a hundred questions. I was in tears. He kept pestering me, asking 'What's wrong with you?' Finally I blurted out, 'I had an abortion.' Immediately the argument was over. He asked me not to leave so we could talk. I decided I could stay for a few hours. We cried together, but could only talk in fragments – we were both so raw and so spent. I left feeling somewhat hopeful that we could work out a peaceful divorce and settlement. But I had misjudged him once again."

Deciding he had been wronged, in retaliation, Frank began telling everyone, including Susan's parents, about the abortion. That caused an unbelievable hurt to everyone involved. Divorce came and went, leaving her with little but the clothes on her back and her beloved Morning Mist. Susan went through the motions of meeting her commitments, but her close friends knew something was dangerously wrong. Feeling alienated from everyone, she felt she could not go on. She strategized her suicide several times, but never followed through. "I survived simply by keeping my exterior mask screwed on tight," she remembers. "The emotional separation I had felt just after the abortion was becoming unbearable. With the passage of each day, I seemed to feel more separated from the me I once was. Some woman inside my body went through the motions of living."

At the time things bottomed out and Susan had no where else to turn, one of her close friends asked if she could pray for her. Thinking it would do no good, Susan agreed, just to please her friend. However, when she awoke the next morning, she immediately knew something had changed. "I wasn't yet free from the pain and guilt," she explains, "but I realized I wasn't consumed with the conclusion that the only way to end my pain was to end my life. In the following weeks I continued to wobble along between relief and self-hatred. My death wish had ended, but I wasn't much beyond that emotionally. Then the same friend who had prayed for me, asked me to listen to a tape about forgiveness. I felt that God could never forgive me for what I had done, but I promised to listen to it. As I ate my solitary meal I listened to the tape, I decided I had nothing to lose by trying to pray and ask for forgiveness. He could deny it, and (I was convinced) probably would. But as I began to pray, I got down on my knees beside my bed and began sobbing. It took three hours before I was emptied. I had no heavenly visions, but something had changed inside me. The hollowness was gone. I felt God had forgiven me, and I could finally begin to forgive myself. I didn't understand it, but I knew it was a beginning. There was a small sliver of hope."

Unfortunately, several traumatic events following her new step toward healing. Morning Mist, who was with foal, had an accident and had to be put down. Susan lost both the mare and the foal. Over the next few years, she moved several times, furthered her education, moved ahead in her academic career, and in 1981 she accepted a position as Academic Dean at a small rural college. After one year, she was summarily dismissed with no explanation. She found herself starting over – again – with a car that was dying, no job, and almost no possessions. In retrospect, Susan believes that the years between her healing in 1976 and the events in 1982 that catapulted her out of her comfortable academic career were preparation for what was to come: the biggest challenge of her life.

"Through studies and case histories, psychologists and medical doctors now know that women who suffer pregnancy losses need to grieve," Susan explains. "Even though I had a doctorate in psychology, I still needed the healing of forgiveness and the opportunity to grieve for my lost child and a chance to bid him a formal goodbye. I knew God had forgiven me, but I was unfinished in my grief work and in forgiving myself. I still needed to put closure to this very difficult part of my life. It was important to me to visualize that aborted baby as a child living in the presence of God in Heaven, loved, happy, and waiting for me to join him someday. I personally needed that to bring healing and peace to my heart.

"Polls tell us that 80% of Americans say that they believe in God. For most women who have suffered the loss of a child from an abortion and believe in God there is a very strong need for them to seek forgiveness. Most women need to seek forgiveness from their god, forgiveness from their baby and be able to forgive themselves. For those women who get stuck in the death and loss of their child, forgiveness and healing allow them to move on with their lives.

"In my practice, with the women who express a belief in God, I ask them to describe what that means for them. This defines the parameters we are working with for this client on our healing journey. Each woman must spend whatever weeks or months it takes for her to work through all her emotional issues around the loss of her child. She must have worked toward forgiving herself and anyone else related to her abortion. Only when these conditions have been met are we ready to begin our final leg of this journey of healing. I ask her to close her eyes and let her mind go back to some memory related to the time of the abortion. Then, slowly, I ask her to envision her god entering the room holding the baby. I have her picture herself back at the scene of the loss, holding the child and rocking it. I ask her to express whatever she feels in her heart as she does this. Always, they are words of love. I love you very much. I think of you every day. I wish this hadn't happened. You are so precious to me. Most women begin to feel an incredibly healing sense of forgiveness and assurance that the child is with God and is loved. I let the women sit for a long time in this peaceful place. There are always some healing tears, but they are very therapeutic.

"Whenever a woman has been through an abortion, forgiveness is a key part to her healing. Otherwise, her grieving process can stay stuck. At times, guilt can be overwhelming and must be worked through. Many women feel they need to seek forgiveness from their child. In many cases the woman has to forgive the father if she felt forced into the abortion, either because she had no support from the father, or the father threatened to leave her if she did not abort the pregnancy. She may have been a victim of a rape which resulted in pregnancy. Sometimes a well-meaning friend who had already had an abortion told her it was no big deal, and then she found out it was a big deal. For whoever was involved in the abortion, the forgiveness of that person is a key element. Every case is individual, and I deal with it that way. We start where the woman is today, and work backward to the place and time of her loss.

"Many post-abortion women who come to me feel unforgiven and terribly self-blaming. I remember one woman who told me, 'I want that healing stuff you do in your book, but can you leave out the God part?' What she wanted was a quick fix, which isn't possible in these situations. Healing is a process, not a one-time only event. People need to process their grief and their loss. Depending on the situation, the research shows that most women suffer one or several of these symptoms after an abortion: unresolved grief, chronic guilt, anniversary depression, psychosomatic illness, drug and alcohol abuse, suicide attempts, psychotic breakdowns, or other lesser resultant effects.

"Most therapists acknowledge the healing power of forgiveness in a person's mental health. There is also a need to say good-bye to the miscarried or aborted child. It is common practice in many birthing centers around the country to allow a mother to hold the miscarried or still-born child (if it is old enough), rocking it and saying goodbye. This provides an extremely important step in the healing process for these mothers.

"We need to be more gentle and loving with ourselves," Susan urges. "If a couple were really looking forward to having the child, and then it never sees life because of miscarriage, then the couple needs to have some healing and bonding time with each other. I have helped many couples take the healing journey together. It often helps them to see their child in Heaven with God. It can ease the pain of their loss.

Susan is often asked, How do we find real happiness in life? "The pursuit of happiness is a four-fold formula: First, if you have a faith, pursue it as a really meaningful part of your life, seeking guidance from your god. Second, ascertain your gifts and talents and pursue the appropriate training and education to maximize them. Third, take the time to be really true to your emotions and honest in your relationships. And fourth, take care of yourself physically, through proper diet, exercise and by using an appropriate way to unwind from the stress of life. The practices of psychologists and counselors are filled with people who are pursuing only one or two of these four avenues to happiness, instead of all four. There is a tremendous need for balance in all our lives."

Author's Note: Susan and her husband, Dr. Vincent Rue, are co-directors of the Institute for Pregnancy Loss in New Hampshire. They have two children and spend their lives helping people heal emotionally. See the Appendix for more information.

Ann Morrison

Delivering Hospital and Community Care with Dignity and Respect

If this is a hospital, then why is everyone smiling? And why is everything so cheerful? Things weren't always that way at Sebasticook Valley Hospital in Pittsfield, Maine. A little over fourteen years ago, there was little reason to smile. There was no pride among the staff, no privacy for the patients, and a pervasive shabbiness welcomed patients and visitors alike.

The hospital had been built in the early 60s to take care of in-patients and obstetrics. There were no out-patient services. The nearest hospital was 25 minutes away. By the mid 70s the small number of resident physicians were tired of being on call for babies who chose to be born any time of the day or night, so the obstetrics services were eliminated. What was left was a 36-bed hospital, with surgery, in-patient care and limited diagnostic services. That seems to have been the beginning of the downward spiral in the hospital's reputation, and it continued downward until the early 80s when it was generally known as a band-aid station. Serious health care facilities were still 25 minutes away.

With that negative a reputation, the revenues were going downhill, also. At the same time, nearby medical centers started to grow. Eastern Maine Medical Center built their tower in 1975. As neighboring hospitals became bigger (and in a lot of people's minds, bigger is better), Sebasticook Valley looked worse by comparison. For the administrator who took over the helm of Sebasticook Valley Hospital next, the stage was set for an uphill battle – straight up.

That person just happened to be Ann Morrison. Ask her what it takes to become a hospital administrator and she'll tell you: "A lot of hard knocks!" Ann grew up in Ohio where she got her nursing degree and then her bachelors degree. "I'm not one who can stay in one place very long unless I'm constantly challenged. I nursed in every department to try to get to know the hospital. I have a real love of learning. I had gone from a 500-bed hospital in Ohio to a 300-bed hospital in the middle of Maine with two 20-bed wards. I thought I was back in the Dark Ages! It was a wonderful experience for me."

The next step for Ann was nursing supervision. "One of the nurses and I went to Baltimore to work in a rehab hospital for six weeks to learn some of the techniques they used. We brought that knowledge back and trained our staff."

That experience boosted Ann into the two-person education department which was strictly nursing in-service. They transformed it into a hospital-wide education department, and brought on another person. "There were a lot of people at Eastern Maine, including my mentor, who allowed us to take risks. That's really important, I think. You don't grow without it."

Ann moved into the Materials Manager position. "I learned a lot about the business of running a hospital and yet I was still involved with patient care. That was my transition into full-time administration. The next logical step was going after my masters degree in business science with a health care finance major. My thesis was on developing a centralized patient transport system, showing how to reduce costs and increase care and put the nurse back at the bedside."

Ann accepted her first hospital administrator job in 1979 at a 28-bed hospital in Dexter, Maine. It seemed that Ann's career was set to go nowhere but up. But the Dexter experience was very traumatic. She had to close the hospital two years later and convince the town that they should become part of a hospital administrative district.

"That was a devastating experience," she remembers. "There were times I made decisions that went against what my boss said. Sometimes I was right; sometimes he was right. But he let me make the decisions and he always supported me. We had to do a lot of public relations and teach the community why it was important to close the hospital before all the resources were bled dry. Often when hospitals have closed in this state they have not been able to give their people any severance pay, have dipped into their pension benefits and their health benefits and the employees are left with nothing. That didn't happen with our employees. That town still manages an endowment that supports health care in Dexter. After a short time at another small hospital, Ann became the administrator at Sebasticook Valley Hospital in Pittsfield. "Things were at a real low in every department at Sebasticook in 1985. We were $500,000 in the red. There were 128 positions. One of the first things I had to do as administrator was eliminate 30 of them. (Not exactly the way to endear yourself to your new employees!) It was a huge percentage. It was not something I would ever want to go through again. There is just no easy way to do that. So we really tightened our belt and now we're really good around here about making the buffalo squeak! And we've been able to turn it around – to the point where we've put on a $4.5 million dollar addition and renovation project that had its grand opening in May of 1993."

With careful, steady coaxing from Ann, the situation slowly began to turn around. "I had learned in other situations to take risks and to let my managers take risks. Each small victory was a step nearer making Sebasticook a model small-town hospital. Two new physicians joined us in July of 1984. One of them is now the medical director of our emergency department. We've added 18 out-patient clinics. We bring in specialists from Waterville, Bangor and Skowhegan. We have a neurosurgery clinic every other week. We have two neurologists who come every other week. We have five orthopedic surgeons who come, as well as a cardiologist, a gastroenterologist, and two urologists. Our local people can consult with them here. We don't do neurosurgery here, but if someone has a problem that involves a neurosurgeon, pre-operative and post-operative appointments can be done right here. That's wonderful for our people."

To turn employee morale around, Ann held quarterly employee meetings to bring them up to speed on things that were happening and then opened the sessions up for questions. It was good for everyone. "There's a spirit in the employees here that is inspiring," Ann smiles. "The staff at Sebasticook are real fighters. They never gave up after that layoff. They just dug in deeper. If you support that in them, they really respond! I'm very involved. I don't sit in this office very much during the day. I do a lot of walking around. I rarely return in-house phone calls. I go to see the person. I think it's very important. That's how you find out what's going on."

Ann has an open door policy. "Anyone on staff here knows they can come into my office to see me. Everyone calls everyone around here by first name, with the exception of a few physicians. Even the patients call me Ann. This is a small town – 4500 people. Everyone knows everyone, so there's no sense pretending you're off in some ivory tower just administrating everything. They know better!"

Made up of nine small towns (Corinna, Newport, Pittsfield, St. Albans, Palmyra, Detroit, Burnham, Plymouth and Hartland), Sebasticook's primary service area serves about 18,000 people. Summarizing the hospital's philosophy, Ann says, "When we embarked on our building campaign, we knew it was important to do more than bricks and mortar. You can put everything in a new package, but if things don't change inside, people aren't going to feel any different. When people walk through our front door, they say it feels different. And it is different. People from other hospitals come to see for themselves.

'We didn't bring in a canned customer service program. I hate canned programs because people can always figure out why it doesn't apply to them. We did bring in a marketing consultant several years ago. He taught us at the management level what marketing was all about. A lot of people in health care don't like that word because they don't like to think of the people we serve as customers. But that's what they are. If they aren't treated well, they won't be back.

"Sometimes we host open houses to get local people in the door. We also hold monthly focus groups of different patient groups and we have 5 or 6 basic questions that we ask them. We tape the answers, transcribe them and share them with the involved departments. That helps keep us tuned into what people want. I don't think there's another hospital in the state that does focus groups quite that way."

Family-oriented health care is very important at Sebasticook. There are no visiting hours. People can come and go anytime they want. If a family member works at night and it's easier to stop in on the way to work, that's fine. If a loved one or friend wants to stay with a patient all night long, it's allowed.

"We also have a pet therapy program. And we don't just let those certified pet therapy animals in. We have some people who don't do well because one of their major family members is a pet that's at home. So we encourage family members to bring the pet in. We haven't had a problem with it yet. We have to be careful that it doesn't get out of hand, but with common sense and compassion, it can be a very important part of a patient's recovery. We have 5 or 6 dogs that are nationally certified. They go through a three-part orientation program where they have to visit the hospital three times before they're allowed on a regular basis. Then they come in once a week and make patient rounds. I think it's a hidden employee benefit, because they make rounds in the departments and the staff just goes crazy over them. Other hospitals have pet therapy programs. It really helps.

"We made sure we didn't move all our bad habits into our new building. We have a grounds committee that makes rounds every month. We really tried to change behavior through our managers.

"We've gone through a team-building project with a consultant and it has moved our organization to the next level. She's been with us six years now and it's the best thing I ever did. Over 100 of our people have gone through team-building. It's not just an in and out thing; we spend six months learning the core concepts and then we have ongoing maintenance. In the next year all 140 employees will have gone through the team-building program. Three of our physicians and three of our trustees, including our board chairman, have gone through team-building. It has given us the tools we need to be better managers. It's heavy stuff. But the trust that is established is unbelievable."

Ann admits that, as good as it is, Sebasticook Valley Hospital is not heaven on earth. One of her goals is to develop a community network. "I'd like to see us teach teambuilding to five- and six-year-old kids. It will be a three- to four-year process where we get all different segments of the community involved. We'll set some attainable target goals so we can build on our successes and go from there. We want to be the impetus, but work ourselves out of a job so the community is a healthy one, meeting its own needs. We're developing systems that help us improve the care we give and reduce the cost to the community. For example, we are developing a CARE management system that will allow us to improve patient outcomes and reduce costs to the payer. We have developed a telephone triage system called After Hours that allows patients to avoid unnecessary emergency room visits. We're also working with seven hospitals to develop our own approach to managed care. The hospital has its own golden rule: We treat others the way they want to be treated. This means we take the time to find out what is important to them."

And the list goes on. Ann has never shied away from a challenge on either a personal or career level. Fear of the future is not an option for this ball of energy and optimism. "I really believe in helping people grow," she says. "It's okay to make mistakes and take risks, because that's how you learn. But we also need to help each other up and offer encouragement when we stumble. As far as I'm concerned, when you stop learning, you're dead. Stop learning and your health begins to go downhill. My biggest personal fear is that I'll retire and not be in a learning mode. So I stay challenged. Work is a very important part of my life, even though I thoroughly enjoy my free time. Life is good, but it's also what you make it. Everyone has difficult situations to deal with, but it's how you handle them that counts in the long run. I always think there must be something even better around the corner, and there usually is, if I'm willing to take a risk. Even a turtle only gets ahead by sticking its neck out!"

Marilyn Paige

Supporting Those Who Care for Alzheimer's Victims

Isolation, fear and hopelessness: these feelings led Marilyn Paige to call a friend — just to talk. These two women shared the common burden of caring for their husbands who had been diagnosed with Alzheimer's Disease. Little did Marilyn know that this one phone call would give her life a mission of reaching out to others to support, encourage and assist the caregivers of those with Alzheimer's.

That was sixteen years ago. "It's interesting," says Marilyn, "that at the time this happened, I had begun to look for new directions in my life. I had always been a stay-at-home mother and an Army wife. When my children were grown, college-educated and starting their adult lives, I needed a new challenge. I had always had my music (playing the organ at church and for local schools) but I needed something to fill the time that I had devoted to my children."

After a marriage of 27 years to a strong, independent and achieving man, Marilyn was told that the memory lapses and inconsistencies of knowledge she was observing in him were symptoms of Alzheimer's disease. They began to experience the early symptoms, and suddenly, she had a desperate need to reach out to others. She contacted a friend who had a family member with Alzheimer's Disease, and experienced great relief at being able to share her burdens and fears. The two women

111

decided to start a monthly support meeting for others coping with the emotional ravages of caring for a loved one with this disease. Different stages of the disease produced different needs in the caretakers.

They stood together, facing down this terrible devastation of the human mind that was besieging their families. Some drove 100 miles to attend the meetings. In addition to caring for her husband, Marilyn began working out of her home to provide people with the names of physicians, sympathetic nursing care facilities, and information about the progression of this disease. Meeting in a local church, inviting speakers who presented the most recent research into the causes and treatment of the disease, and providing leadership and hope, Marilyn quickly became a recognized authority on family issues and Alzheimer's disease.

"At that first meeting, I knew I had found my life's mission," she smiles. "It was meant to be." That devotion has helped hundreds of families cope with the ravages of Alzheimer's disease. Her efforts have sensitized physicians to the needs of families, promoted sympathetic and professional respite care programs, and provided much needed dollars for research. Ten years from that first support meeting between Marilyn and her friend, the Maine Chapter of the Alzheimer's Association hired a professional executive director. The organization provides support for Alzheimer's families, funds research, develops respite care programs, trains family and professional caregivers and provides volunteers to any Maine family who needs assistance.

Alzheimer's Disease is called the disease of the 1980s because that is when it became more widely known through the efforts of people like Marilyn who sought to educate the public, ask for support, and provide information and help. The disease has been around for years, usually mistaken for the normal aging process. This debilitating mental disorder that strikes four million Americans is much more than normal aging. It is the destruction of brain cells which causes not only harmless forgetting, but a cruel and capricious loss of vital functioning. One out of 10 people over the age of 65 and a small percentage of people in their 40s and 50s are affected with Alzheimer's.

Caregivers for victims of Alzheimer's Disease witness a wide variety of behaviors brought on by this disease. Sometimes it's the inability to take care of personal hygiene, or the aimless wandering, or the hostility brought on by the frustration of not knowing how to do any of life's simple tasks. Caring for an Alzheimer's victim is an arduous task, likened by many to a 36-hour day. This phrase became the title of a book by Dr. Peter Rabins and Nancy Mace describing the hard work and sacrifice demanded of caregivers and family members of Alzheimer's sufferers. The disease is hard on the victims in the early stages because they seem to be aware that they're forgetting things and getting confused. But it is just as destructive to caregivers and their families. Half of all patients are cared for at home by their spouses, adult children or other devoted family members. Because of consciousness raising, there is now more support for these families through visiting nurses, respite care volunteers and other programs. However there is a serious toll to the caregiver. Problems range from trying to keep a wandering patient out of harm's way 24 hours a day to finding day care and long-term care facilities.

In 1988 Marilyn was honored with the Jefferson Award, given annually to people who have devoted their resources and their energies to the service of others. She was also the recipient of The Better Life Award, given by the Maine Health Care Association in recognition of her outstanding achievement in making the lives of Maine's Alzheimer's families more manageable.

Marilyn Paige did not give up when it would have been easy to do so. She turned her personal tragedy into a means of helping others persevere through difficult circumstances. Nor did her commitment end with her husband's death. Like any nonprofit organization, the Maine chapter has several annual fund-raisers, and she's often there, helping raise the money to provide resources and encouragement to the family members who suffer right alongside the Alzheimer's patients they're caring for. She's also Mom to 42 Alzheimer's support groups, serving on various committees, and occasionally speaks to groups who want to know more. It's not unusual to find her volunteering with the nitty gritty details of running the local office. She still counsels families in their homes and many come to her for information and support. Always looking for new ways to help others who are hurting, she also volunteers once a month at a local soup kitchen and has formed a support group for widows.

In 1995, Marilyn was named the State of Maine Mother of the Year. Her gracious and selfless personality, coupled with her wise and compassionate counsel, make this woman a joy to know and a friend to all who need her.

Her search for a new life mission, her selfless giving to the caregivers of Alzheimer's victims and her perseverance in the face of adversity have enriched the lives of thousands. Because of her hard work, Maine is on the cutting edge of care-giving for Alzheimer's patients and serves as a model for other states in developing the kind of services needed. If you have a loved one with Alzheimer's, because of Marilyn Paige, there is help — and hope.

Beth Reese

Bringing the Joy of Books to Homeless Children

It's been said that the secret of success is finding a need and filling it. If that's true, thousands of children in northern Virginia would call Beth Reese a smashing success. Beth is the founder of The Reading Connection (TRC), a volunteer organization that takes books to homeless children. "There are many people trying to help homeless families," Beth explains, "and we didn't want to duplicate their efforts. Families who have lost their home for one reason or another need food, clothing and housing, of course, but literacy is a gift that lasts a lifetime! Often the help that's provided is a band-aid, meeting the necessary and urgent needs. For the

children in these families, being homeless is a scary experience, one they'll remember all their lives. If we can give them something good in the midst of all the misery, it makes life a bit easier."

Beth's own childhood was happy and full of wonderful books. "I always had people in my life who supported me in following my own dreams. That makes all the difference. I always had some project going on, even organizing carnivals and giving my toys away as prizes. And I always knew I was going to be a teacher. It was a natural outlet for my creativity and entrepreneurial qualities. I love to start things, but I'm not so crazy about finishing the details! I'm much better at motivating others to get behind an idea and carry it through. Because my husband shares my dreams and goals and enables me to be home with my kids, I have a lot of time to volunteer. I can't imagine not being involved in making my community a better place. No one does community service alone. It takes a lot of people working together to make an idea work. My gift is being able to articulate a vision so that people will take it and run with it."

In 1988 Beth served on the outreach committee of the Greater Washington D.C. Reading Council, an organization for teachers and educators. Beth thought a great way to reach out to the community would be to encourage the area's homeless children by sharing books with them. "Most people are very surprised that there are thousands of homeless children in northern Virginia, just five miles from our nation's capital. These families are homeless because there's a shortage of affordable housing."

The Reading Connection is a literacy outreach program for homeless children living in shelters. The program is a read-aloud program, encouraging reading by sharing books, rather than by teaching skills and repeating drills. Beth, who holds a masters degree in education with a reading specialty, explains. "Before you can learn to read, and before you can decode words, you have to have been filled up with language and the knowledge of books. Otherwise those funny symbols on the page won't mean a thing. That exposure to words happens naturally for most children, through seeing books and magazines and newspapers in the home, and having special adults in their lives read to them. The children who have trouble with reading are those who may not have been shown that books are treasures. A lot of kids can learn the letters, but they don't understand the joy of reading. If the person reading to you has joy in the voice, you want to make the connection between the printed words and the ideas transmitted. Reading to kids is the main factor in building a reader. The rest is secondary.

"What's so wonderful about reading to kids is that it's the foundation. Everything the child craves – undivided attention, the shared experience, the intimacy – is in the reading together experience. We must not underestimate the importance of reading aloud to children. It's a life-changing event."

The Reading Connection reaches over 1000 children a year in several homeless shelters. Usually the homelessness is acute, rather than chronic. The Connection's volunteer readers visit shelters that are relatively short term, where the residents are almost always women with children, most of them single moms. Statistics show that this is a growing population in our country. Most of them are homeless through no fault of their own. The homelessness might be the result of an economic crises or domestic violence. "Half of the homeless people in our area are children," Beth says.

"These kids are often bounced from school to school as the mothers move from shelter to shelter. They don't have the opportunity to be children. They're looking for escape and adventure, so they leap on any chance you give them to do that. That makes this whole project fun for the kids and for us, too."

Almost 90% of the books are donated to The Reading Connection. All the books they give away are free to the children. There are four parts to the program: Giving the child experience with books. Volunteers visit the homeless shelters once a week and read to small clusters of children. If it's possible to draw the parents into the experience, they do. Giving the child ownership of books. Every child receives a bag with new-quality age-appropriate books and reading and writing materials. Giving the child access to books. A small lending library of hard-cover books is set up in each shelter. It's usually a cozy corner where the whole family can go to read. Giving the child membership in a free book club. As they leave the shelter to set up a new home of their own, the parents can sign up for the book club. They receive mail at their new address and they can choose two books a month for each of their children, absolutely free. To date, everyone to whom the offer was made has chosen to join the free book club, putting over 1000 books into the hands of the children.

"Homelessness has no color," says Beth. "The families we serve are equal numbers of white, Hispanic and African-American. On the first visit, the children are given a book bag with four or five appropriate books. They write their names inside the covers of the books and each week we add to their personal library. They take them with them when they leave the shelter. Can you imagine what it means to a homeless child to have something of their very own – with their name on it – especially when they have just lost the most basic necessities of life? We're very picky. If you're only going to own six books, they'd better be in good shape! It's like Christmas when we give out those beautiful, top-quality books!"

Reading to children is not just a diversion. It's a wonderfully intimate time between parent and child – a time when personal values are learned and bonds are strengthened. The value a parent places on reading is evident to children, without the parent saying a thing. If children never see their parents reading for enjoyment, never experience the pleasure of snuggling while sharing a book together, they will not perceive reading as a fun activity. How they perceive the importance of reading can change the direction of their lives. If parents allow reading with their children to be pushed aside by the tyranny of the urgent, their children's lives will be affected. Think about it. Where would you be if you couldn't read, or if you saw reading as just something you have to do in daily activities?

In 1989, Beth began with ten volunteers going to read to the children in one shelter. The second year, they received funding through a grant, enabling them to expand the program to other shelters. By 1992, Beth had a waiting list of volunteers and shelters were calling constantly. Realizing this project was only going to continue to expand, Beth pursued nonprofit status and The Reading Connection became a nonprofit corporation, so donations could be tax-deductible. Now they are receiving funding from corporations, foundations, United Way, and individuals. There is no government funding involved. From a first-year budget of $1,000, TRC has grown to an annual budget of over $100,000.

In 1996, The Barbara Bush Foundation for Family Literacy gave TRC a grant. "You can't serve children without serving the family, too, and they wanted to know how we were going to reach the mothers and encourage them to continue reading to their children after they left the shelters," Beth remembers. "It made us start new ways of reaching the mothers. We asked them what would help them continue reading to their kids. They had plenty of ideas, and plenty of questions! One of the things we did was provide information on what types of books are appropriate for which age groups. We began to offer workshops on how to read aloud and how to write a story with their kids. If their English skills aren't strong enough, we show them how to use picture books to have a reading experience with their children. Parents want their kids to do well in school, so they are very open to learning what they can do to help. Many of them never had the opportunity to be kids themselves. When we color with the children, they color, too. That's a wonderful experience for both of them!

"Some of them call us and talk about how their kids are doing in school after they're back on their own. The relationship we've built with some of these mothers is very rewarding to us. They give us feedback, and we give them lots of tips on reading as well as reading charts they can put on their refrigerators."

Beth insists that this is something anyone can do. "We wear jeans and sit on the floor and read to them. By reading and sharing books with the children, they also learn to read, and to view books as treasures. Hopefully, the homelessness is a temporary crisis, but these kids are at risk of falling through the cracks permanently. We provide a service to them during the crisis time. If we can hold them up and give them the resources, maybe we can save them from losing too much ground academically. Being read to is not just an academic exercise. The positive interaction for the families is the most important piece of this project. When you are under stress, dropping everything and reading to a child is a real relaxer! It's an escape for both of you, a learning adventure. And you're touching and snuggling, not yelling or fighting.

"Children don't understand the crisis you're in. You've lost your home, and you're feeling like a bad mom. This is at least one thing you can do to ease the hurt and confusion. It's a very powerful thing, yet, it's so obvious people miss it. It's free. It's simple. Kids love it. Tutors can't do this for you. You need to do it. If you read to your children every day, they will excel.

"I believe in my heart that everyone has potential and value," Beth explains. "Everyone is my superior in some way. People in shelters aren't losers; they're winners. After all the obstacles they've overcome, their families are still together, caring for each other, making short- and long-term goals. I admire their strength and I learn so much from them. Bringing the joy of reading to these children is one of the greatest joys I've ever experienced. The other fun part for me is watching people enjoy their volunteering. None of us gets paid, but we all get rich beyond belief!"

Beth Reese has a passion for community service. She believes women should use their gifts of nurturing to extend a helping hand to those who need it. "There's always someone you can help," she says. "If you care enough about something, someone, somewhere will help you do it. I believe, as Marion Wright Edelman said, *Service is the rent we pay* for living."

Nancy Savage

Making The House Into a Home for Families with Sick Children

For Attorney Nancy Savage, "Let's go home" means Ronald McDonald House. Last year, Nancy gave up her law practice to become the first house manager for the new Ronald McDonald House in Portland. Why in the world would she do that?

Nancy grew up in Massachusetts, graduated from Georgetown University with a degree in history, then worked in banking for three years, and then moved to Portland in 1988 to attend University of Maine Law School. After graduation, she worked as an associate attorney with a local law firm until her move to Ronald McDonald House. "I really enjoyed practicing law," she says. "I left because after three and a half years, I felt a need to put something back into the community. I've had a great life and I'm enjoying it very, very much. I've always wanted to give something back because of the abundance I've received. I've done some of that through the years, but it wasn't enough. This was an excellent opportunity to do something more. I really

looked at it long and hard because doing something like this is one of those things you think about doing someday. At that point in my life I had no commitments, no family, no house to tie me down, so it was the perfect timing for me. That was the spring of 1994, and I read about the new Ronald McDonald House and the need for a house manager.

121

"I just knew that was my job. There was no question in my mind that this was what I was looking for. The administration part of the job and working with people as well as the public relations aspects of the work here are all things I love to do. But most of all, it was a great opportunity to give back to life what had been given to me. The timing was perfect for me. I still pinch myself every so often to prove that I'm really here!"

The very first Ronald McDonald House opened in Philadelphia in 1974 as the result of the perseverance and dedication of Fred Hill, then a Philadelphia Eagles football player. After their daughter was treated for leukemia at the local children's hospital, the Hills became determined to help other families faced with the same situation. Very few institutions at that time provided sufficient accommodations for such families, and Dr. Audrey Evans, a pediatric oncologist at Children's Hospital, suggested that a home away from home was needed.

"Hill enlisted the aid of his teammates and the local McDonald's restaurant franchises to raise the funds to purchase and renovate the first house. He asked the Philadelphia-area McDonalds for a portion of the proceeds of their St. Patrick's Day Shamrock Shake promotion. He was told the project could have all the proceeds, if the house would be called Ronald McDonald House. One McDonald's executive explains, "We named it Ronald McDonald House because we felt that kids would feel a bit better knowing their parents were staying at Ronald's house.

By 1979, 10 more houses had opened. In the next five years, 60 more opened their doors and today, there are 190 Ronald McDonald Houses providing temporary housing for about half a million people a year throughout the United States, Canada, Asia, Australia and Europe.

Each Ronald McDonald House is unique, created by a team of local citizens to meet the needs of their community. The house is owned and operated by a not-for-profit organization established by local concerned citizens. Before a commitment is made to develop a house, several key elements must be present: medical advisors from a hospital with a need for such a house; a parent organization, often comprised of parents whose children have been treated or are being treated at the same hospital; interested and concerned volunteers; and the support of local McDonald's restaurant franchisees.

Ronald McDonald House is the cornerstone program of Ronald

McDonald House Charities. Established in 1984 in memory of McDonald's founder Ray A. Kroc, RMCC awards grants to not-for-profit organizations throughout the world to help children live up to their fullest potential. These grants develop and encourage programs in the areas of health care and medical research (including Ronald McDonald House), education and the arts, and civic and social service programs.

As the president of Ronald McDonald House International Advisory Board says, "Just when the family needs to offer all of its strength to the child, the simple demands of everyday life seem overwhelming. Worst of all, the sick child knows it. He can read the exhaustion of his mother's face, see the fear in his father's eyes, and feel the pent-up energy of a younger sibling who hasn't had a chance to run or laugh or play with other kids for weeks. What's really tragic is that the burden this places on the sick child often hampers the success of his treatment. Parents of sick children need others to listen and care, and they can't find that kind of support in a hotel. Children receiving outpatient treatment for cancer can play in the house without being self-conscious about their crutches or bald heads. Parents can share news about their child's diagnosis. And the families' healthy children can have fun with the other children staying at the house."

Everyone who works at the house has one purpose: to soften the edges of the trauma hitting the families who shelter there while their children are ill.

"Our house is a warm and sunny place, filled with and staffed by loving, caring and giving people who have gone above and beyond for the families here," says Nancy. "It's a place filled with love and hope, not depression and gloom. Of course, there are those times when the reality of a terminally ill child overwhelms the parents and they lose it. At those times, there's little anyone can do or say. I just cry with them."

Hundreds of local businesses and thousands of individuals worked together to get Ronald McDonald House of Portland ready to open in May of 1995. From banks to grocery stores, restaurants and dairies, sign makers and soap producers — help came from everywhere. And not just from adults — many children sold cookies and lemonade or ran garage sales and donated the proceeds. It takes over $180,000 a year for operating costs to make the house a home. Think about what it takes to

123

run your household — mortgage or rent, groceries, utility bills, cleaning products, furniture — and then multiply it times 15 guest rooms and an office and you'll have some idea what's involved. When someone opens the refrigerator for a snack, or opens the door to their room, something has to be there! "This is a very special place," Nancy smiles. "It was built by people from all over Maine, not just by the Portland Community. We can be very proud of what we've done together. This is truly 'The House that love built....'"

As in all professions, it's difficult to watch people suffering without being affected yourself, Nancy says. "The burnout factor is something I worry about. I don't want to burn out, because I love my job. I want to make this house a success. Let's face it, I've been dealt a hand that's hard to lose with! So one thing I do for myself is go home and have time with my family. It helps me keep my perspective and refreshes me. Time away makes me better able to do my job here. There are cases that tug at my heartstrings, of course. It's hard sometimes to keep from getting too involved. I probably err on the side of being more involved that I should be, but I can't help it. That's who I am."

There are constraints to Nancy's job which most of us wouldn't want to live with. For example, she has a 9 P.M. curfew on weeknights. That means that if she goes out, she must be back by 9 to be available as the volunteer coverage ends and the families come home for the night. If she wants to stay out later than 9 P.M. she has to find a sitter for the house. It's much like being a single parent.

Nancy's spirit of giving is the benchmark of her life. She also serves as President of the Board of Directors at Goodwill of Northern New England and an American Red Cross Pheresis Donor.

Nancy has goals for the house, as well as for herself — a list of things she wants to accomplish. "I hope to offer a lot more services for the families, such as making more meals available to them here at the house and at local restaurants."

The 200+ volunteers fall under Nancy's supervision. There seems to be no end to the creative ways to help. One of the most interesting is the Guest Chef Program. She explains, "People who like to cook just volunteer to come and cook dinner! They either use what we have here and bring the rest, or bring the whole meal themselves. One of our guest chefs is a mason by trade, so when it's raining, he comes and cooks for us. We have a wonderful guest chef coordinator/volunteer. It wouldn't do to have three guest chefs show up on the same night!"

About 90% of the families who stay at the house come from Maine Medical Center; families with neonatal problems, and cancer and cardiology problems make up the majority. But sickness cuts across all levels — intellectual, financial, emotional, and social — and the families who stay at Ronald McDonald House all have one thing in common: a severely ill child. That's what bonds them together.

"The children don't always stay in the hospital; sometimes they stay at the house with the family. It they're here for outpatient therapy or preadmission workups, there's no need for them to stay at the hospital. It's not uncommon to have both sick and well children playing together in our playroom. Everyone is in the same situation, and everyone understands. It's a very nurturing atmosphere," Nancy explains.

"I don't do counseling as such, because I'm not a trained health professional. I do the administration and supervise the volunteers and try to keep tabs on what's going on with families. As they come home at night, I sometimes make myself available to see how they're doing. If they want to talk, we do. I just try to be caring. But I do work closely with the social workers at the hospitals, so I'm aware if things are not going well for the family and it helps me do my job. I can steer them to the right agencies if they need help. I'm a referral source for them.

"It's very fulfilling for me to be here at this time in my life. This is a small thing I'm doing to try to make the world a better place. I hope I'm making a difference for people. Sometimes parents who stay here don't have the energy to cope with all they face, so I see children who sometimes need hugs. I hope someday those kids will remember that there was a lady in Portland who cared enough about them to give them an encouraging hug when they needed it.

"What this place is about is taking people who are under a huge amount of stress and making it a little easier. I do whatever needs to be done, whether it's making the soda machine work or shoveling the driveway if there's no volunteer to do it. No day is the same here. No two families are exactly alike. But they all need one thing: someone who cares and a house to call home."

Nancy Savage believes you have to have aspirations. She says, "I had a dream and I went for it. That sounds a bit corny, but I believe it. The question I wanted to answer is not *Am I going to give something?* but rather <u>*What*</u> *am I going to give?*"

Jane Marston

Raising Money for Disadvantaged Animals

Kevin Costner danced with wolves, but Jane Marston dances with horses. Very special horses. Royal Lipizzans, known for their grace and beauty and their formal classical equitation. Once you've seen them, you'll never forget them. They don't perform; they dance.

Like a lot of her girlhood friends, Jane took basic riding lessons, and promised herself she would own a horse of her own someday. Then, after seeing the Disney movie, *The Miracle of the White Stallions*, no horse would do for Jane except a Royal Lipizzaner. It was many years before her dream was fulfilled. After earning her degree at Bates College, Jane's career path led her to teaching, and then public relations, and eventually into her present position, Marketing Director of Medical Mutual Insurance Company of Maine. It's a good fit, because when you meet Jane, you know she's very involved in her profession. "My position with Medical Mutual is certainly the most enjoyable of my career," she enthuses, "I'm working with a team of astute physicians and health care and insurance industry professionals who are committed to both product integrity and superlative service. I could not be more motivated to market their message!"

Jane brings that same enthusiasm to her avocation: proclaiming the greatness of Lipizzans. Because of their great love for all animals, Jane and her husband, Don, volunteer tremendous amounts of time and energy to arranging shows for the Lipizzans to benefit local Humane and SPCA groups. Jane explains, "It just seems right, somehow — animals helping animals. The shows are usually great successes, sometimes raising as much as $18,000 to help feed and house disadvantaged animals."

What's so special about Lipizzaners? Jane's love for these special animals is evident as she shares their history. "The breed was begun in 1564, the year that Shakespeare was born and Michelangelo died. They are a combination of the great Spanish Andulusian horses (holdovers from the Roman warriors) and Arabians, known for their extreme beauty and exquisite bone conformation. They are very intelligent and are known for their wonderful dispositions. Even the fiery stallions have gentle temperaments. The stallions are widely known because their heavy musculature and great strength allow them to perform the celebrated ballet-type forceful leaps and plunges known as Airs Above the Ground. In the 16th Century, the powerful Austrian Imperial Court, under Archduke Charles, established its own breeding farm at Lipizza (in what became Yugoslavia). Named Lipizzans after the town of their origin, they became the greatest war horses in the world. Bred for the exclusive use of the Hapsburg royal family of Austria and the military aristocracy, they became the proud ancestors of the Lipizzans we see today."

During the 50s, 60s and 70s, Lipizzaners were not sold, they were somehow mysteriously acquired and bred. All pure bred Lipizzans can trace their roots back to six dominant stallions whose strong bloodlines became the brilliant basis of this rare breed. These six famous stallions were: Maestoso, Favory, Siglavy, Pluto, Conversano and Neapolitano. Throughout their 430 year history, there have never been more than 3000 Lipizzaners in existence at any one time. Today there are fewer than 600 pure bred Lipizzans registered in the United States, and between 2,000 and 3,000 in the world.

There were almost none. During World War II, the Lipizzan mares were in what was then Czechoslovakia, about to be seized by the advancing Russian Army to be used as ordinary war mounts, or worse, for food. In June of 1945, through a series of small miracles, General George Patton put the Spanish Riding School, and the Lipizzaners under his protection, and the Third Army rescued the Lipizzan mares barely in time, reuniting them with the stallions and saving the breed from extinction.

In the 1960s, Colonel Ottomar Herrmann, Sr., brought his herd of Lipizzans to the United States. Lipizzans have been in the Herrmann family for six generations, a period spanning nearly three hundred years. Today, Colonel Otto Herrmann (son of Col. Herrmann, Sr.) maintains a ranch in Florida to help ensure the continuation of the Lipizzan breed. His Lipizzan stallions have performed throughout the United States, Canada and South America.

Jane had met Col. Herrmann in 1971 when he first brought his Royal Lipizzan stallions to Maine. Since her father was an editorial writer at a local newspaper, she asked if she could scoop the special interest story on the horses. She was at every performance and interviewed not only Col. Herrmann, but his family as well — not once, but several times! "I became an immediate sycophant," she laughs. "I was a Lipizzan groupie! I followed them all over the Northeast and was at every performance I could attend. The Herrmanns were very gracious to me. We've been friends ever since."

Enamored of the gentle and beautiful Lipizzans, Jane finally convinced Col. Herrmann to instruct her in classical equitation on the Lipizzan stallion, Marcus Favory. "Marcus is a lap-horse," Jane laughs. "He would cuddle in your lap if he could figure out the logistics of it!" Jane was Col. Herrmann's last private student, and Marcus is now retired at Col. Herrmann's ranch in Florida.

It wasn't until 1996 that Jane finally was able to fulfill her dream of owning one of these beauties: a magnificent Royal Lipizzan mare named Birgetta Maestoso. If you can imagine a silvery-gray panne velvet body with peachy-pink muzzle and lush lashes framing deep, licorice eyes – that's Birgetta. And it's love at first sight for everyone fortunate enough to meet this 22-year-old Lipizzan mare whose pedigree goes back to 1898. Birgetta has given birth to six foals in her lifetime and is now ready to enjoy the good life of retirement. Jane and Don are devoted to providing that for her. "She's a sweetheart," says Don, a retired professional actor whose career included touring with Lana Turner and Eva Gabor, among others. He adds, "We spoil Birgetta unashamedly; she gives us so much pleasure."

129

Lipizzans are famous for their beautiful pearly-white color, a mark of status and privilege for their royal owners and riders. Although they are born black or dark brown and only very gradually turn gray with age, a Lipizzan may not turn fully white until the age of five to seven years. They are also famous for their amazing Airs Above the Ground, those incredible leaps and plunges performed only by stallions of exceptional strength and intelligence. It takes about three years to learn the movements which predate the birth of Christ by 400 years and are derived from defensive horsemanship created for war. These maneuvers were originally meant for use by mounted soldiers to inspire terror in the hearts of foot soldiers. It's hard to look into the gentle face and deep dark eyes of a Lipizzan and imagine its being used to terrorize anyone, but in the Airs Above the Ground, the horses' bodies were used to protect the riders from being wounded. Imagine being a foot soldier in the 16th century and suddenly, right in front of you, this 1100-pound massive white stallion, ridden by your enemy, hurls his body straight up into the air and kicks his back feet straight out behind him — all four feet off the ground at once! The foot soldier would have died of heart failure, if nothing else!

Jane uses her marketing and public relations savvy to provide care, food and shelter for animals less fortunate than her beloved Lipizzaners. "It's a wonderful marriage of privileged animals helping disadvantaged animals. Animals are among the most helpless in our society. We all have a responsibility to do whatever we can to help those who have no one to care for them properly," she says. The Marstons are also strong supporters of the Flying Changes Center for Therapeutic Riding in Topsham, Maine, a school where developmentally and physically challenged children are introduced to the pleasures of riding and being friends with horses.

"My parents were very involved in the community and encouraged me to do the same," Jane remembered. "Both my parents instilled in me the belief that I could be anything I wanted to be. I think we all should take our abilities and see how those skills can help others. It's networking — connecting the dots of life — taking one group or individual who needs help and connecting them with a group or individual who can help. That's when two parts make a much greater whole. My goal is to give people a greater awareness that their local animal shelters really need their help and support. You don't have to own an animal to do the responsible thing and support an animal shelter. Who knows? You just might end up with a wonderful four-footed companion and friend!"

Rosie Hartzler

Teaching Young People Skills for Living a Productive Life

They're the forgotten. They're 16 to 24 years old and they've slipped through the cracks. Some have been abused, neglected, or thrown away. Some have no home, no job, no education. Some are single parents trying to make it on AFDC. But they're smart. Street-smart. And wise in the ways of the world, far beyond their years. They're the young people who live on the streets. And they're right in our backyards.

That's what prompted Rosie Hartzler to take the teaching position at YouthBuild, a segment of Maine's Portland West Project which is designed to revitalize and restore the West End of the city.

Raised on a farm in Ohio by her loving and supportive Mennonite family, Rosie knew she had the gift of teaching, but it didn't become clear until later that her skills included patience, a sense of humor, compassion, dedication, vision, and tenacity — all qualities she would need in her teaching assignment at YouthBuild.

One of six children, Rosie learned a solid work ethic very early doing farm chores. After graduation from Goshen College with a degree in Physical Education, Rosie faced a dilemma. She didn't fit the Mennonite ideal for women, because physical education was not a typical career for a woman. In spite of that, she taught phys ed for 12 years in a Mennonite high school that had a progressive attitude toward

133

integrating its students into the world. "I was allowed to do a lot of innovative things as a teacher and a coach," says Rosie. "But the time came when I wanted to give up the coaching and just focus on creating curriculum so that every young woman in that school could find some physical activity she liked and could continue it after high school. I think people should find a way to enjoy the gifts and talents they were given. A lot of my curricular innovations are still being used there. That's gratifying to me."

After earning her masters' degree at Temple University, Rosie felt it was time to move on to a new challenge. She decided to go to seminary, where she came to a deep personal reconciliation of who she was as a woman, and what she had been taught while growing up. The result of this personal struggle was an evolving epiphany that the two were not incompatible. After seminary, a close friend of Rosie's was asked to be the chaplain at the University of Maine. Rosie went with her, looking for the next phase of her life, whatever that might be.

"I'm coming to my teaching now with a whole different perspective that can only be gained by living for awhile," explains Rosie. "I realized I didn't want to teach high school phys ed anymore, so I began taking courses to earn certification as an elementary teacher. Looking to the Portland area where there were more opportunities, Rosie found a position teaching phys ed for grades K-5. "I had a ball! But the person who was on medical leave that year came back, and I was out of a job again. It was at that point that I saw an ad in the paper about YouthBuild."

YouthBuild is a project funded by the U.S. Department of Housing and Development (HUD). It is the idea of Dorothy Stoneman who started the first program in East Harlem. Now there are 100 YouthBuild sites around the country. The program has been in Portland for four years, and comes under the umbrella of Portland West Neighborhood Planning Council. The goal is to enroll about 30 young men and women, 90% of whom are high-school dropouts with low income. About one third of the students are women. Some students are parents. A certain percentage need to be in low-income housing and a certain percentage need to be receiving AFDC. They are a culturally diverse group, ages sixteen to twenty-four. The goal is twofold: to increase their academic skills and earn their GED (Graduate Equivalency Diploma), and to acquire some vocational skills as the group renovates low-income housing. The students spend one week in the classroom, then one week on the jobsite, alternating back and forth for the nine months they are in the program.

The group has renovated several local buildings. The process is basically to gut the building, reframe it, install sheetrock and finish the interior. One project was an apartment building in which some of the YouthBuild graduates were the first tenants. They are justifiably proud of their work, and the skills they've learned are invaluable.

"There is nothing in my teaching background that prepared me for the challenges of this job! Absolutely nothing," Rosie laughs!

The student body usually numbers in the 30s at the beginning of the year, with graduates numbering around 20. "Unstable housing is the number one reason for attrition in our program," says Rosie as she shakes her head. "Even the 16-year olds have been on the streets. Very few of the students live with their parents.

"These young people are the ones who didn't fit the mold in high school. They're the ones who just couldn't hack a run-of-the-mill, you-must-fit-in-this-box type of schedule. So they quit."

Rosie has dreams for the future, both for herself and for YouthBuild. "I would like to see the age limit raised from 16 to 18. A sixteen-year-old knows he or she doesn't have to settle in yet or get serious about the business of living. And they can't get the GED until they're 17 anyway, so they have less incentive to really take the program seriously. And, strange as it may sound, at 16 they really haven't had enough time on the streets yet to get really tired of that lifestyle. They don't know enough yet to know what they need to make it as an adult. At eighteen, they are more serious about the program."

Rosie's face lights up when she talks about teaching. It's obvious she was born to this profession. There's that light from within that spreads all over her face and animates her hands and body language as she describes methods she's tried with the young people that have worked.

"I was a good student myself," Rosie remembers, "and to be teaching a group of students who have challenged me on every assignment, and have become very angry at me when I asked them to do an assignment, has not been easy for me. But it's been very rewarding. The biggest thing I had to learn was that their reactions had nothing to do with me, and everything to do with them. I had to give them the room to rebel.

"I really believe in the importance of good communication skills, so I was determined to find a way for each student to increase his or her level of writing and speaking skills. I believe that these students know a lot. But they don't know that they know. And they have no confidence in their ability to put what they know on paper. So I introduce the concept of writing right on the computer very early. It eliminates the pencil and paper. We start with word processing. Of course, some people feel more confident with that pencil in hand. That's okay. I just want them to get outside themselves.

"One of the first attempts I made at integrating writing and social studies was when two nuns were murdered in a nearby city. Each of my students was asked to choose one person who was there — the nun in the kitchen who heard the screams, the neighbor across the street, the police officer who first arrived on the scene — and write from that person's standpoint. How did she or he feel? What went through the mind of that person? It was a powerful assignment, and produced some outstanding work. I don't want to teach them only how to produce good grammar; I want them to produce literature.

"March was women's month," she says. "I had been reading the New England Woman magazine for months and I got the idea of using the cover stories for teaching role models. I asked for and received a complete set of the magazine's back issues and had the students read the articles and discuss the qualities the cover women had that qualified them as role models. [Little did Rosie know her request was going to land her on the cover of the magazine as well!] I also used articles from MS. Magazine. Then I asked the students to write their own "Woman of the Year" article about someone they knew. It was a great exercise for them.

"Then we tackled the welfare system as a subject. All these students are products of welfare, but my focus was how to get off welfare. We took in a lecture at the university; and we had speakers come to the class. I was amazed at the rage these young people have on this subject! It supports my theory that they know a lot. But the gaps in what they know are scary. For example, they know a lot about money; but they can't put together a simple budget. There is a small stipend that each student in the program receives, which gives them a start toward fiscal responsibility."

Teaching is not a one-way street and Rosie readily admits how much she's learned from her students. (She's also learned to sheetrock and pound nails!) The YouthBuild program lasts only 9 months. "It's not enough," Rosie moans. "We want to place these students in jobs that are hopefully going to bring them more than minimum wage and get them off the system."

There is an application process to get into YouthBuild. The students have to be highly motivated, because it's their choice to come to YouthBuild. Getting the GED is a big incentive, of course. Another is the small weekly stipend they receive while they're enrolled in the program.

"We're now a State of Maine alternative school," Rosie says. "I'd like to see us become a lot more intentional about integrating our curriculum, so we don't just have the students out on the jobsite for a week. These are really important skills. But while they're on the jobsite, they're not doing any reading or any writing or learning to integrate both sides of this educational coin. I'd like to see us come up with a way to do both the vocational and the intellectual at the same time, to integrate them, so it's not just one thing and then the other. We need to find a way to do both.

"I love problem solving. I enjoy using my creativity and helping others use theirs. The students know I'll be honest with them and will always expect them to live up to their potential. It's important in teaching to also be a learner, and I can honestly say I've learned a lot from these young people. I want them to trust themselves and have self-confidence. They have so many reasons to not believe in themselves, but they need that self-confidence. If they have that, they can do anything!"

Rosie Hartzler has a passion for helping young people live up to their full potential. What could be more important to a person's future than that? Teaching is a calling, and Rosie is definitely called — to share her knowledge, her enthusiasm, and her love of life with kids who have been forgotten by most of their community. She puts these kids first, something most of them have never had before. That kind of commitment pays off, for the kids under her tutelage, and for Rosie herself, in the rich reward of knowing she has made a difference in the lives she has touched.

"This past year was the most creative, energizing and productive year for the students at YouthBuild," Rosie enthuses. "We did some innovative integrating of subject matter, including researching the history of the house we were renovating, a Victorian Second Empire structure. We also were able to utilize local literacy volunteers for our reading/writing program. I love finding a way to empower people to achieve their full potential," she says. "That's not only my biggest challenge in teaching, but it's also my biggest personal reward." That's probably why the class of '96 voted her the *most enthusiastic and persuasive* and the class of '97 recognized her for the ability to *push us past our limits.*

Thalia Jillson

Breaking Through The Stained Glass Ceiling

Nothing rains on Thalia Jillson's parade...not 46 years of being married to a paragon of dermatology, not raising three daughters, not breast cancer, not ecclesiastical red tape...*nothing*.

Thalia is part traditionalist, part free spirit, and total inspiration. Her roots go deep into New England Congregationalism; she was raised just twenty miles from Plymouth Rock. She inherited her positive attitude from her parents – her mother graduated from Mt. Holyoke in 1914, and was a scholar and active suffragette, and her father was an insurance salesman, during the Great Depression! (That takes a positive attitude!) "I grew up in genteel poverty," she laughs. At age sixteen she enrolled in the premed program at Tufts University on full scholarships.

The very first week, she met her future husband on a blind date. Named for the town where he was born, Otis Field Jillson told Thalia if they married, she'd have to spend the rest of her life in Maine as a country doctor's wife. Just before graduation, he emphatically and unequivocally stated that "one doctor in the family is enough." Like almost every other woman of her generation, Thalia said, "Yes, Dear." For practical financial reasons, only one of them could go on to medical school, and in those days, the norm was for the man to pursue further education. They married one month after they both graduated from college, in 1940. "He got his M.D., and I

139

got my P.H.T. (Putting Hubby Through)," she smiles. There is no resentment in her voice. That's just the way it was. Their first daughter was born in Bangor, during Dr. Jillson's internship. Nine days after completion of the internship, he was off to the war, while Thalia established a home base. Those were not easy days. Not only did she have a new baby, she was pregnant with their second child.

After the war, the Jillsons moved to Hanover, New Hampshire, where Dr. Jillson served as a professor at Dartmouth Medical School, and later, Chief of Dermatology at Mary Hitchcock Memorial Hospital. They were there for eighteen years, followed by another eighteen years in Bangor, Maine, practicing dermatology. Thalia, with her staff of five, ran the office.

"I did all the right womanly things," Thalia reminisces. "In addition to raising my daughters, I worked outside the home, was a deaconess in the church, and was very active in many civic affairs, but I always had this yearning for learning – for wanting to live up to more of my potential. I knew there was more out there for me."

When the Doctor retired in 1985, the Jillsons did all the things they hadn't had time to do before. The next summer, after three days of chest pain (for which, perversely, he refused to see a doctor) Dr. Otis Field Jillson died in his sleep of a heart attack.

Suddenly, the future lay wide open and beckoning to Thalia. Like so many women who have always been someone's daughter, someone's wife, or someone's mother, when Thalia found herself no longer Doctor Jillson's wife she asked herself, Who am I? "How could I have done otherwise?" she explains. "When set adrift by his death, searching for what I would do with the rest of my life, how could I do other than face the issue of my own identity?" As she read the writings of other women struggling with the identity issue, she found that she was not alone.

"To some, the quest comes late; to others, never. I have discovered the basis of my aspirations, rooted in the desire my mother gave me to fulfill my greatest potential. I hadn't thought much about being a woman, my own woman," she says. "My voice had been stilled for those forty-six years in a cocoon of domesticity, nurturing, rearing three daughters, working closely with my husband in his practice of medicine, and submerging my original aspiration to become a doctor myself. It was after my greatest loss that I started on the path of renewal. I grasped a lifeline of hope and aspiration, pursuing a graduate degree in Adult Education, concentrating in Gerontology."

At 67, Thalia Jillson enrolled as a graduate student at the University of Southern Maine. At age 70, she received her Master's Degree in Gerontology, "a discipline," she says with a twinkle in her eye, "in which I had a head start by virtue of my age." It was precisely 50 years since she had earned her bachelor's degree.

Her courses were to be a means to an end: grief counseling, for which she felt an affinity. But she "found the process more fulfilling than the goal; it is in the journey rather than in the destination.

Along with her studies, she worked with Widow to Widow and did a lot of reaching out to others who were suffering grief and loss, because she felt it was a good way to help herself through her own grief process. Following graduation, she began leading workshops on grieving, and speaking on the joys of aging. What started as a course in death and grieving to help herself adjust to her widowhood, became three years of night school, hitting the books, cramming for exams, and term paper deadlines. You would think that would be enough for someone who had already lived a long, full life. But it wasn't enough for Thalia. In 1994, at age 74, Thalia Drake Jillson, received her second graduate degree: Master of Divinity from Bangor Theological Seminary.

Religion is still a male-dominated field (even though the number or women clerics has tripled since 1977): only 10% of full-time clerics are women. (From Working Woman, July 1995, p. 40). What made her take the road less traveled by women – the theological path to often predictable career oblivion?

"Something was missing," Thalia explains. "There was an aching inside that told me I wasn't doing all I could do, that I wasn't giving all I could give. In 1991, I went to a pilgrimage retreat for personal renewal. One of the things we were encouraged to do was write out a conversation with God, stating how we felt, and how we thought God would respond. I was overwhelmed with a sense of unworthiness. I poured out my heart on paper and the dialogue just wrote itself. I had a sense of God's presence and acceptance of me as a minister. In that experience, I received what I consider a real call to the ordained ministry."

Thalia enrolled at Bangor Theological Seminary to get the training she needed. For three years Thalia hit the books, commuting to Bangor for her courses, staying in a small apartment on campus. (Wouldn't you just have loved to be a fly on the wall in some of those student jam sessions where Thalia held her own with those kids right out of undergrad?) She now serves on the Board of Trustees at Bangor Theological Seminary. Her perseverance paid off. But she still had to exercise her faith, because she could not be ordained in her denomination until she had a group of people who wanted her to minister to them. Until that happened, she could not be addressed as "Reverend."

"In my mind," she explains, "my call to the ministry in 1991 meant the ordained ministry. (Ordination is the rite of investing a person with ministerial functions in a particular denomination.) In my denomination, you have to have theological training and a congregation that wants you as its minister in order to be ordained."

After waiting for a year and a half, Thalia's home church voted to establish an outreach ministry to the elderly. There was only one logical choice to fill the new position, and they extended the following call:

The First Parish Congregational Church, United Church of Christ, in Gorham, Maine, hereby extends a call to Thalia Drake Jillson, subject to ordination, to become Minister of Outreach to:
 1. offer the sacraments of the church.
 2. counsel with those who express need.
 3. visit with a pastoral concern.
 4. lead groups or individuals in worship services.

This official call to ministry was the missing ingredient in fulfilling Thalia's dream. Thalia went through a 5-month process and on May 12, 1996 (Mother's Day) she became The Reverend Thalia Drake Jillson, ordained by God – and the church.

"Since then, I haven't had time to breathe!" she laughs. "I conduct services on Monday nights at the local retirement home. I also fill the pulpit for area ministers when they are away. I visit shut-ins and serve them communion and have an active pastoral counseling schedule. I've performed weddings, funerals and everything in between and I absolutely love it! I knew back in 1991 that this is what I was meant to do. It just took me five years to get here!"

Will she ever slow down? "Not until my brain fails me!" she replies. "I'll never be finished." Thalia believes that "no years that prepare us for and lead us toward our goals are wasted. It is in the journey that we live, not in the destination.

"We all go through losses in life. And we grow through losses. In my 77 years I've been through a lot, and I feel I have a lot more to give. What sustains me is my sense of being called. I don't think God would have brought me this far to drop me now. There is a great sense of peace and fulfillment in doing what you believe God wants you to do, even if it's just waiting. I believe that you're never too old to help others, and that God is always there for us."

In the midst of her daunting schedule, in the spring of 1997, Thalia was diagnosed with colon cancer. Within days she had surgery, which was successful. A few hours out of recovery, she requested her hearing aids and a telephone; there were people who needed her. Thalia's dedication to helping others and her compassionate nature, coupled with that irrepressible sparkle of humor make her a much beloved minister and friend to all who know her. Her children call her *Reverend Mom.*

What is there inside Thalia Jillson that made her use her own brokenness and grief to help other people over the same hurdles? She learned from her mother's example that helping others was a fulfilling way of life; her husband was in medicine, one of the helping professions; she had a mastectomy; and she is a cancer survivor. Helping others is Thalia's credo and way of life.

Losses
by Thalia Drake Jillson

Oh faithless, Fate! I pledged my answer
Never to say "Why me" and swore
When first I lost a breast to cancer
My faith would even up the score.

143

My private tears were shed sans sadness,
No pathos rained on my parade.
My sunrise shared exceeding gladness,
"This is the day the Lord hath made!"

The loss of journey long awaited
With family to a far-off land
By fostering love was compensated,
Life's larger goals to understand.

Fate, I can forfeit all I cherish
And walk away, nor look behind,
But oh, I pray, lest I should perish,
Dear Lord, don't take away my mind!

I mourned the passing of my mother,
I nursed her through the lonely night.
The inborn privilege we could proffer
To die at home as was her right.

Then came the years of empty nesting.
Three daughters one by one depart,
Each with a mate her life investing,
Each a void leaving in my heart.

Oh fickle Fate, you still weren't sated.
My senses slowly slipped away.
The thundering symphonies abated,
My vision dimmed from rose to gray.

With Milton at his blindness railing,
How could I not respond in kind?
Beethoven's hearing sadly failing –
But Lord, please let me keep my mind!

Then came the time to lessen labors,
To lighten loads and rest our souls,
Departure from our roots and neighbors,
Consolidation of our goals.

A part of us we left behind us:
Identities, ambition, youth.
Which path would let our future find us,
Which trail would lead us to our truth?

Our lives we planned around each other.
We said, "Grow old along with me,
For this forsaking father, mother,
The best of life is yet to be."

But gentle sleep can last forever.
Death's silent stealth a way can find
My dear love's bond of life to sever.
Oh Lord, how can I keep my mind?

He left me in the midst of living.
He walks beside me all my days.
Life is not taking, life is giving,
And not for me to curse the ways.

The wounded heart in need of suture
With scars from past bereavements joins.
Each loss gives strength to face the future,
Each sadness girding up the loins.

I weigh my heartaches, sorrows, weeping,
I count not losses, only gains.
Life's in the waking, not the sleeping,
And joy the balance tips 'gainst pains.

Oh Fate, thou took my dearest treasure,
To lonely loss I am resigned,
But left me life's abundant measure.
Dear Lord, Thou spared my soul and mind!

Dr. Melinda Molin

Pioneering New Support for Women with Breast Cancer

Breast cancer, unfortunately, has become a fact of life. But the dreaded diagnosis doesn't have to ruin your life – or end it. Thanks to people like Dr. Melinda Molin, there is not only hope, but help in surviving this disease of epidemic proportions which threatens one out of every nine women you know.

Trained as a general surgeon, Melinda took specialized training in surgical and intensive care in Hartford, Connecticut, and in trauma surgery in San Diego. A native of New York City, Melinda was approached by Maine Medical Center to move to fill a position as a trauma and critical care surgeon. When she arrived at Maine Medical Center in 1990, she was the first and only woman M.D./general surgeon in the Portland Area at the attending level.

Because trauma surgery requires intense time commitment and availability as well as tremendous skill and expertise, Dr. Molin was doing all sorts of general surgery at all times of the day and night. Women and referring physicians began to seek her out because many of the patients felt they would have a level of comfort with a woman doctor regarding breast issues that they might not have with a man, no matter how

147

competent. She was not specializing in breast cancer; she was just seeing more and more women with breast problems in her regular surgical practice. Over the years, it became about 95% of her practice. Women from Northern Maine, New Hampshire and even Vermont sought her out when they found a lump or had an abnormal mammogram.

"I couldn't be sitting in the office with a woman who had driven hundreds of miles to see me and get a call that I was needed to operate on a car accident victim in ER," she explains. So she moved from trauma and critical care surgery. "Nothing is ever lost," she says. "I consider myself fortunate to have had the experience in trauma and critical care, but my interests were evolving into caring for women diagnosed with breast cancer. Breast cancer is an epidemic. 25% of women who are diagnosed with breast cancer will be dead within 5 years. It's a devastating diagnosis, not just for the woman, but also for the family. The entire family needs all the physical and emotional support they can get.

"The first question I ask my patients is, 'What is your understanding of why you're here today?' Even if she's here only because her mammogram was slightly abnormal, almost every woman who comes to me has herself already dead and buried – no matter what. My way of getting to ground zero is to ask what she understands about her situation. As she opens up and talks to me, I can gauge the amount of information she has and how she is processing it, and what her level of anxiety is. Then I can tailor what happens during the appointment so that when a woman walks out my door, she has information and optimism."

Ever mindful of the fact that people process information differently, Melinda asks her patients at the outset how they want to be told the results of their tests. Some want to know the worst right away. Others want to receive the news over the phone, while they're at home alone, whether it's good news or bad news. Others want to come into the office and hear it in person, and maybe bring a good friend with them. This gives the patient some feeling of control on some level in a situation that appears totally out of her control. Many have said the worst part is the waiting – for the results of a biopsy, for the doctor to schedule treatment, for the confusion to go away and a positive plan of action to take hold.

For many years, Dr. Molin had a dream. She envisioned a multi-disciplinary breast center in the Portland area. She tried to work on bringing the vision to fruition by herself, but it wasn't until one of the women administrators at Portland's Mercy Hospital became a patient of Melinda's that the idea of bringing all the different doctors and resources under one roof became a reality. "That woman didn't have cancer after all," smiles Melinda. "She only had to have the biopsy. But that meant she had to run between the anesthesiologist, the radiologist, the surgeon, the pathologist, the nurses.... It convinced her there needed to be a level of excellence and integration to make it all work. She asked me how we could put it all together. Portland's Mercy Hospital gave me the opportunity to fulfill my dream, and I jumped at the offer. In January of 1996, The Breast Health Resource Center at Mercy became a reality. My office is right here in the hospital now, and the staff and administration are extraordinarily supportive. It's a marvelous opportunity for me to really make a difference for our patients.

"Through the Breast Health Resource Center, we have greatly reduced the waiting time between one specialist and another, or one procedure and another. And the woman herself is not having to make all the phone calls and set up the appointments. All she has to do is come here and meet with them.

"There's no question that women and men think differently. One of the ways that women get from A to B is by not going from A to B. Women have the same conversation with the same information half a dozen different times with half a dozen different people until the decision is made to their satisfaction. Our Nurse/Coordinator at the Breast Health Resource Center, Cathy McDonald, is an incredible person and a marvelous resource for these women.

"Many of them call her and she's always there for them – to talk, to give information, mostly to listen. Yes, it's part of her job, but with her it's much more than that. She's really in it with them. She can hear the confusion in their voices and can usually recommend which specialist they need to go back to for more clarification. No one is left hanging out there by herself. It's great working with such a well-trained and dedicated group of medical professionals. It sounds corny, but we all really do care."

The Breast Health Resource Center at Mercy has its own administrator and a nurse-specialist. Specialists are brought to the Center as they are needed to consult with patients. Most women don't need every specialist. The Patient Education Center has books, videos, computer access, a conference room and wonderful resources to help the patients understand their diagnoses and treatments.

Dr. Melinda Molin doesn't pull any punches with her patients. If she has a concern, she says so. She's a no-nonsense, professional woman who has the courage to face the tough issues head on. Her own fortitude and positive attitude do much to help her patients face their situations with calmness and faith. Her expertise and skill give her patients the facts and options they need to face a difficult diagnosis and determine a course of action. In all of this, she balances professionalism with compassion. She is both an encourager, and an encouragement to all who are fortunate enough to work with her or be under her care, including the families of her patients.

Lest we give the wrong impression, it's not just specialists from Mercy Hospital who participate. The Resource Center is located there, but it's a resource for the entire three-state area. Specialists from other hospitals make the time to come to the Resource Center to consult with patients. There's a good spirit of cooperation in the entire health community, and the emphasis is on the patient's comfort level, not the convenience of the medical professional. And that's the need that Melinda saw that motivated her dream.

Because she is vision-driven, and a very articulate and persuasive advocate for breast cancer patients, the Breast Health Resource Center is a reality today. It is used not only to consult with patients, but weekly multi-disciplinary educational conferences are held there as well. It's an opportunity for the professionals to discuss actual cases and ask each other questions – the radiologist, the oncologist, the surgeon, the mammographer – all the people who swing into action when a breast cancer diagnosis is made. Everyone learns and, ultimately, the patients benefit from the shared knowledge.

What drives Melinda Molin? People's needs, whether they are perceived needs or unperceived. For example, she discovered that no one was doing anything to help patients with lymphedema, a condition where a limb will swell and experience a degree of impairment, due to the removal of lymph glands in breast cancer surgery. Melinda started a

150

lymphedema treatment program.

She adds, "I always felt that in the treatment and care of breast cancer survivors some of the pieces always fell through the cracks. One of them was the psycho-social support group. There are support groups out there, but no one seemed to be addressing the needs of the spouses and families. Any trauma, whether it be a severe accident or a diagnosis of breast cancer, acts as a watershed for a family. There's family life *before* the trauma, and family *after* the trauma. A family gets through the surgery and the chemo and all that, but then what? No one seemed to be tackling a couple's issues following breast cancer, including sexuality issues. And those issues definitely exist, whether they're acknowledged or not. They need to be discussed and brought out into the open. Husbands need to know that other husbands have the same thoughts and questions. The wives need to express their fears and feelings in front of the husbands. Breast cancer is not like having cancer in your toe! It affects the entire life and every relationship the survivors have. They all need to know they're not alone. To give that support, we have started a support group for couples, facilitated by mental health professionals. We had a 12-week pilot program and the results were extremely rewarding, so we have moved ahead with it. Some parts of the program are insurance reimbursable.

"I get teary-eyed when I talk about this," Melinda laughs self-consciously. "Revolutions do not come only from without; they come from within. This entire Resource Center and the support groups and all the great things that are happening – these are a revolution. We still don't know what causes breast cancer. Current thinking is that most occurrences are caused by a combination of genetic predisposition and other factors, such as dietary, environmental, and psychological. The good news is that the majority of women diagnosed with breast cancer who have treatment will be alive and disease-free in ten years. And 80% of all biopsies are negative. So the best thing a woman can do is get that mammogram, do that self-examination, get that biopsy if your doctor orders one, and follow his or her prescribed treatment. The absolutely worst thing a woman can do is wait."

Because of the dedication of doctors, researchers and cancer survivors, there is hope for women and men diagnosed with breast cancer.

The diagnosis is a horrible jolt in itself, but because of Dr. Melinda Molin's compassion and foresight, some of the peripheral agony has been eliminated for the patients under her care. For that, we can all be grateful.

Nancy Schoch

"Cuteness definitely counts," says Nancy Schoch, a West Highland White Terrier breeder and owner of Windsong Westies on Cape Cod. There is nothing quite so adorable as a wiggly, tail-wagging, white ball of fluff with licorice-drop eyes and nose who can't get enough of your attention. But, sad to say, there's such a thing as being too cute. Westies are often bought for their adorable looks and new owners are often taken aback by the strong will and hunting instinct of the breed. With Westies, cuteness can be their downfall.

"Any type of terrier can rule the roost if it hasn't had proper training as a puppy. Terriers are extremely intelligent and stubborn and must be raised like an extremely bright child," Nancy explains. "Owners need the discipline to discipline their dogs and set behavior boundaries."

Nancy operates the Westie Rescue organization of Cape Cod. Nancy first got involved in Westie Rescue in 1985. She had been breeding West Highland White Terrier champions and showing them since 1973. To date, she has finished six of her champions (they gained their titles.) Her dogs normally produce two to three litters a year.

Almost every recognized breed of dog has a rescue organization. When dogs are abandoned, or dropped off at animal shelters, the volunteers in the nonprofit rescue group for that particular breed pick up the dogs, bathe them, and have their temperament and health checked. They socialize them, if necessary, give them any training they need and crate-train them. Then they find them a good home. It sounds straightforward, but there's a lot involved…and it's not all pretty.

Doberman Pinschers, for example, are often purchased because the owners want a macho dog. Then they torture the animal to try to make it mean. Dobies are gentle and stable dogs, and teaching them to be mean just doesn't work, so the owners abandon the dogs, or take them to the veterinarian to be put down. Reputable vets and shelters will not put a healthy dog down, but will make every effort to find it a good home. Rescue volunteers have heard every excuse in the book for not wanting a dog any longer, including that the owners got new carpets and the dog's color no longer matches their color scheme. (Hard to believe, but it has happened.) Usually, though, the problem is that people don't understand the breed of dog they've purchased and it just isn't what they expected. Expectations are often completely unrealistic. Other reasons for surrendering a dog range from allergies, behavior problems (often lack of training and discipline on the owner's part, not the dog's), divorce (where neither partner wants or cannot keep the dog), and long-distance moves where it is not possible to take the dog. With Westies, it could be breed-specific skin problems that require more medical care and expense than the owner can handle.

Nancy has traveled as far as 200 miles to pick up a Westie in trouble. Westie-oriented dog lovers all over New England are on the lookout for candidates for rescue, scouring the classifieds for free Westie ads, keeping in touch with their local animal shelters, and keeping their Westie antennae alert. When they find one, they call Nancy. "I keep a rescue Westie as long as it takes to find a proper new home," Nancy says. "I evaluate the dog first, and accumulate as much information from the owner or the shelter medical records as possible. Is the dog afraid of thunder storms? Where does it normally sleep? Anything that will help me find a good match. Then I bring the dog home with me. I have a veterinarian do a thorough checkup – immunizations up to date, heartworm test, and neutering or spaying if that hasn't been done.

"I have an active list of people who are interested in having a Westie. It's normal for me to get 4 to 5 calls a day from people who are interested in puppies, or rescue dogs. I interview the potential adoptive parents very thoroughly, and educate them about the breed and that particular dog. I spend a lot of time putting the match together. The happy ending is when a rescue Westie goes to its new home, accompanied by a folder containing all its medical and personal information. I keep in touch with all of the adoptive families with periodic phone calls. I tell them, 'Call if you have any questions or problems. If the dog doesn't work out, no matter how long you've had it, I'll take it back.' Evaluation, rehabilitation and placement can take from one week to four months. The best possible family match is the goal. The adoption contract specifies that if they cannot keep the dog, they will not put it in a shelter or give it to someone else. So far I'm batting 1000. I've placed as many as 17 rescue Westies in one year. So far, none has had to be rescued a second time!"

There are two major reasons people give up Westies: Westie-specific skin problems and biting (nipping at a toddler, biting the UPS man, or biting the husband who gets back into bed with the wife after the dog has been sleeping on the husband's pillow while he was on a sales trip). A lot of people feel guilty about giving up their dogs. In some cases, they probably should never have had the dog in the first place.

"People look at these cute little white animals and think they're adorable lap dogs," Nancy explains. "But a West Highland White is a terrier, bred to hunt and kill mice and rats, for example. Westies are very bright, and very opinionated. They are bred to react quickly, so they don't need humans to tell them what to do. In the Scottish Highlands, farmers often had a pack of hunting terriers to rid the farm of vermin. Since Westies are pack dog oriented, they tend to want to take over the family pack. This is a trait peculiar to terriers; they're very independent! If a family has several small children, they might discover the Westie nipping at their heels, making them do what the Westie thinks they should do! Some breeds need more training than others to get along with people and children. Training is key for the first year. If more people actually trained a Westie puppy properly for the first critical year, we'd have fewer dogs ending up in rescue because the owners couldn't cope with the dog, or didn't understand the breed."

It's more than dedication to the breed that makes Nancy do cartwheels to rescue a Westie in trouble. "I'm a stubborn Scot," she laughs, "and this breed came from the western highlands of Scotland. So I have a natural affinity for them, anyway. Aside from that, these are bright, intelligent, reactive dogs who can sense your moods and be excellent companions. And to be perfectly honest," she smiles candidly, "it's hard to get much cuter than a Westie puppy!"

Why do rescue volunteers do it? It certainly isn't for the money! All the cost of housing, feeding and healing the dogs are paid by the volunteers out of their own pockets. Often, like Nancy, the rescue volunteers are breeders themselves. Nancy sums it all up with her own raison d'être: "If I don't rescue him, who will? I'm not afraid to get involved. It's a small price to pay for the love these loyal little dogs have given me. I can't save the world. So I save Westies."

The Story of One Rescue Westie
©Nancy A. Schoch. Used by permission.

Molly's story started in August of 1990 when she was found wandering in a small Cape Cod town. The requisite ten days in a concrete cell at the pound passed with her being unclaimed. Fortunately, an alert member of the WHWTCNE (West Highland White Terrier Club of New England) read about her in the Adopt-A-Pet column of the weekly newspaper and, after much red tape, we arranged to adopt her. Molly had extremely bad skin, was covered with fleas and sores and, with wisps of gray and yellow hair, bore little resemblance to a Westie. But we saw a glint of her latent personality which encouraged us to salvage her rather than mercifully destroy her. She was spayed, medicated, bathed incessantly, given a hypo-allergenic diet, and most importantly, lots of love.

Two months later, a wonderfully bright, affectionate Westie with the beginnings of a shiny white coat was placed in her new home. Shortly after that, we received a letter from her new owner saying, in part:

This report will be so favorable it's hardly credible! The vet

156

agrees that it's unbelievable that anyone could throw Molly away. She's perfectly housebroken. She sits nicely on command and we will start down, sit-stay, and down-stay this week. As soon as she can pass all, she can go into the Companion Animal Visitation Program at the nursing homes with me. No one can believe what heartless souls discarded Molly. But she sure got lucky and so did we!

And as a postscript to Molly's success story, in March 1991, she became a Certified Therapy Dog with, incidentally, some of the best obedience skills I've ever seen in a Westie!

Caroline Morong

Making Wishes Come True
for Children with Life-Threatening Diseases

"When you wish upon a star, makes no difference who you are!" Jimminy Cricket's mellow tenor voice croons comfortingly, encouraging us all to dream big dreams and look optimistically to the future. That's hard to do when you're twelve years old and you've lost all your hair because you have leukemia. Then you meet Caroline Morong and suddenly life is fun again.

Caroline Morong was the first president of the Maine Chapter of to Make-A-Wish Foundation. How she came to be Maine's premier fairy godmother is a story in itself.

One of six children, Caroline grew up in a loving, nurturing environment in Connecticut. After earning her associate degree in nursing, Caroline settled in Camden, Maine, where her family had a summer home.

"I really loved nurturing children and trying to make them feel better when they were sick," she says. "Kids don't carry around as much garbage as we adults do. Their innocence and courage are very inspiring.

"As a young woman, I went through that normal growing up stage where you party all the time. But I didn't know when to stop. When you get involved in drugs and alcohol, you lose a part of your chronological perception. Whole pieces of your life are fuzzy or just missing. Realizing what I was losing, I went to rehab, joined AA and turned my life around. I've been sober now 15 years, which is really exciting to me."

Married to Wayne Morong, a local Camden businessman, Caroline very much wanted children of her own. Having a stepson helped, especially when her own pregnancies ended in miscarriage several times. After many, many years of trying, the couple was blessed with their first child, Luke, in 1987. She attributes the successful pregnancy to getting free of the alcohol and drugs, because all the doctors and tests never found any reason for her inability to carry a baby to term. All was not well, however. Luke had been born with no esophagus. Surgery in the neonatal unit of Maine Medical Center corrected the situation. Six months later they discovered he had a leak between his esophagus and his trachea, causing food to go into his lungs. Again the condition was repaired, and he has been fine ever since. After waiting so long to have her own child, and then going through these medical traumas, Caroline has a tremendous empathy for parents with sick children.

"This whole experience changed my life profoundly. Luke didn't have a chronic illness, but the whole thing devastated me. I was very scared, but I had an amazing amount of support from family and friends, for which I'm very grateful."

Two years later, Caroline's daughter, Laura, was born very healthy. About two years later, the couple's third child, Liza, was born with underdeveloped lungs. Again, they rushed to Maine Medical Center and after four weeks of intensive medical care and a new miracle drug, Liza was fine. And still is. "I don't think there's anybody better at what they do than the pediatric doctors and nurses at Maine Medical Center," she says. "Seeing children struggling everyday just to live with diseases such as cystic fibrosis and cancer, made me so very grateful for what I have in my own life. My niece was diagnosed with leukemia at 18 months. It tore us all apart. (She's been in remission for seven years now and doing great.) My gratitude just grows every day.

"At that point in my life, I had never heard of any of the wish-granting organizations who work with children with life-threatening diseases. One of my friends told me about Make-A-Wish and suggested I might want to get involved. The minute I heard about it, I responded positively. I knew this is what I wanted to do. Before this time, my husband had been seriously injured in a very bad car accident. It was a very long and grueling recovery period and I remembered how the community and friends reached out to help me at that time. Make-A-Wish seemed like a good way for me to give back some of what had been given to me.

The Make-A-Wish Foundation of America was established in Phoenix, Arizona, in 1980 and is the nation's largest and oldest wish-granting charity, with over 80 chapters in the U.S. as well as international locations. It is supported by over 8,000 volunteers. It all began with a seven-year-old little boy named Chris Grecius who had leukemia. Touched to the core with Chris' condition, his friend, Tommy Austin, asked him, "If you could be anything in the world, go anywhere you wanted to go, or have anything you wanted, what would it be?" Chris responded, "I want to be a police officer."

Tommy Austin had a lot of friends at the Department of Public Transportation and Safety and through them he arranged for Chris to be a Phoenix police officer for one day. They gave Chris a helicopter ride all over the city and had a uniform tailored to his size, including a badge and a cap. His assignment: to issue parking tickets. Shortly after that wonderful day, Chris Grecius lost his battle with leukemia. At the end of his short life, the only thing he wanted at his bedside was his police uniform. This one experience inspired Tommy Austin to start the Make-A-Wish Foundation.

Since Chris Grecius had his wish to be a policeman fulfilled, over 35,000 wishes have been granted. In the two years since Caroline organized the Maine chapter, 125 wishes have been granted to Maine children with life-threatening illnesses.

Wish referrals can be made by the child's physician, social worker, health care professional, parents, legal guardians or by the child directly.

A Wish Team then visits the child, learns from the child what his or her heart's desire really is, and then plans the details and makes the wish happen. The idea is to provide the Wish Child and his or her family with special memories of joy and laughter at a stressful time in their lives. A wish offers a respite, a time away from the strains of dealing with a serious illness. It's a family time and the entire family takes part whenever possible. All wish expenses are fully covered. The average cost of fulfilling a wish is around $3500.

Wishes are limited only by the child's imagination. About 55% of the children want to go to Disney World. But Make-A-Wish has fulfilled wishes of every variety imaginable, from building a fishing pond in a backyard, to sending a child around the world to meet a special person. Make-A-Wish has never turned down a wish for an eligible child.

Having a wish come true is magic for a child. For parents, it's a time to create a new memory...one that just may have to last forever.

How is all this financed? Make-A-Wish is totally nonprofit. Caroline draws no salary. Her reward is the smile of a child and knowing that she has helped make a difference in that life.

Granting a wish requires immediate cooperation from dozens, sometimes hundreds, of people and organizations. This is the time when a major airline may quickly provide plane tickets for the family, or a celebrity may change a busy schedule to meet a special child.

Many times fulfilling a wish means racing against a deadline — the disease's deadline. "It's difficult for a parent to pick up the phone and call Make-A-Wish because by doing so, they feel they're admitting the child doesn't have long to live. Often, they wait too long, and then the child is too ill to have his wish come true. Sometimes we've had to wait for a child's disease to go into remission, or wait for his or her strength to be built up, or wait for the results of a test. It's frustrating, because the clock is ticking, waiting for no one."

Maine is a large state when you have to travel from one end to the other, but the Make-A-Wish people cover it all. They have volunteers from all walks of life, of all ages, who share their talents, services and monetary contributions to transform a youngster's fantasy into a magical moment of reality. To nurture the happiness of children who must bear the burden of illness just as they begin to dream is Make-A-Wish's reason for being. The children themselves are eloquent.

I have always wanted to see the ocean...Mommy says it's beautiful. Please can I go?

Guess what — sometimes I forget I am sick. Sometimes I even forget I have cystic fibrosis, and even though I have spent most of my life in the hospital, sometimes I can forget that. My VCR helps me forget. Thank you for it and making it possible for me to pick out the films I want to watch. I hope you can help other kids get what they wish for, then, maybe for a little while they will be able to forget their illnesses. That is my wish for them. P.S. These are my words, but my mom's handwriting. My I.V. is in my left hand, the one I use to write with.

In a special fund-raiser at malls throughout the state between Thanksgiving and Christmas, Make-A-Wish displays beautifully irresistible playhouses that kids can win in a drawing. The program is called Playhouse '98 and the playhouses are donated by local lumber yards and builders. To own a playhouse is a dream of many children, to Make-A-Wish children are no exception. Many people work together to make the Playhouse Program a success, usually raising over $20,000 a year for granting wishes.

Charitable contributions are Make-A-Wish's only means of financial support. Of every dollar donated, 84% goes directly towards fulfilling wishes, with 16% paying for fundraising expenses and administrative costs and supplies. When you give to Make-A-Wish, your money goes where you intend it to. This is one organization that does not use telemarketing, so if you get a call from a wish-granting group, please know that it is not to Make-A-Wish. Caroline and the Board of Directors insist on the highest integrity in all their operations.

There are limitless ways you can help make a wish come true for very ill children through Make-A-Wish. There are different levels of giving, of course, and they are explained in each newsletter the organization sends out. Once a Wish Child is referred and the child's parents contact to Make-A-Wish, the child's physician has to qualify that child as having a life-threatening medical condition. A team of two volunteer Wish-Grantors goes to the child's home to determine what the child's wish is. No promises are made until they are sure they are able to grant the wish. On this initial visit, the volunteers always take flowers and other ice-breaker gifts for the child's parents and siblings as well as the Wish Child. After the Wish Team ascertains that the wish really is what the child wants, they shift into high gear to plan the wish. No detail is hurried over; everything is planned carefully to make the child's dream a reality.

The philosophy is to never say no to a qualified child's wish. Fortunately, most wishes fall into four major categories: I want to go...I want to be...I want to meet...I want a....

Individuals and companies are contacted who are in a position to help make the wish fulfillment one of the happiest and most memorable events in the child's life. Only one wish is granted to each wish child, so it's important to get it right. Finally the wish becomes a reality. But it doesn't end there. The Wish Children and their families stay in touch long after the wish has been granted.

But being a prototype fairy godmother has its pitfalls. It's hard to stay uninvolved emotionally. It's difficult when you've worked hard to make a wish come true for a very sick child and then the child is too sick to have his or her wish granted. That's very hard to accept, because everyone is geared up and ready to make the wish come true. Caroline explains, "You find yourself thinking the if-onlys and that can tear you up if you let it. This is my job; it's what I do. Like all working moms, I find it can be difficult to balance my own family life with the demands of my work life. That's when my family really shines. My husband will say to the children, 'Now, kids, this is what Mom does and it makes her happy. She helps a lot of sick kids be really happy, too, so we need to share her a little bit.' He's wonderfully supportive of me. It means a lot. Considering that my kids are all under 10, they've been very understanding, too."

The first year Make-A-Wish existed in Maine, Caroline and her group granted six wishes. The next year it jumped to 44. The number of wishes has been increasing every year. The flip side of that coin is that there are at least that many children under 18 with life-threatening diseases.

If Caroline Morong could have anything she wanted, what would it be? "My fondest wish is that we go out of business — that there would be no children to whom turning 18 is just a dream. That would mean we had triumphed over childhood illnesses." Jimminy Cricket, are you listening?

Kim Block

Delivering the News with Responsibility and Compassion

Many people use the Yellow Pages to hunt for a job, but it's not usually by sitting on them! But that's how Kim Block – who is no stranger to anyone in Maine or New Hampshire – got her start in TV. With a degree in broadcast journalism, Kim began her career at radio station WLOB in Portland, Maine.

Her senior year in college, Kim met the new general manager of WLOB in Portland. They became friends and he offered her a job at the station as news director in 1978. Then she made the move to WCSH radio

and then WGAN radio, which was owned by TV Channel 13 (WGME). After a year, Kim had met many of the reporters for WGME and she decided to audition for the first job that came along in the TV station. She told the news director of her eagerness to audition. The first position that opened up was the 6 o'clock news anchor.

She set up an audition interview, but he didn't seem to take her very seriously. Four times they set an audition time, four times she rearranged her work schedule at the radio station, and four times he canceled, meanwhile flying in would-be anchors from all over the country to audition for the open spot. After all, she was just the kid from the radio station. Finally, five-foot-one-inch Kim Block stood in front of the man's desk and said,

"Just because I work down the hall, doesn't mean I shouldn't have a chance at the anchor position. You really need to give me an audition." His response was, "Okay. Let's do it right now."

With no time for preparation – or for jitters either – she found herself in front of the TV camera with a teleprompter in front of her. The studio didn't have adjustable chairs at the time, so Kim was too short for the desk when she sat behind it. They gave her the Manhattan phone book and Yellow Pages to sit on. Never having even seen a teleprompter before, she was concentrating all her effort on doing a good job when the telephone books she was sitting on slipped and she slid right under the desk – the camera rolling all the while. She pulled herself back up and kept on reading from the teleprompter, acting as if nothing had happened. The crew was doubled over with laughter, but she made it through the audition to the end. The news director said, "If you can maintain your composure in that kind of a situation, you can probably handle almost anything that might happen." She got the job.

Now, you need at least three years of on-air experience to land a position in front of the camera. "I was in the right place at the right time," she laughs, "even if I **was** sliding under the desk!"

In December, 1998, Kim will have been the TV news anchor for 18 years. That must be a record. She's had opportunities to move to other stations, but she's turned them down. "This has become my home," she smiles. "A large part of that feeling is because I really do believe it's important to give back to the community. That is one of the most satisfying aspects of this job. There are so many opportunities to help people."

Kim lends her name and her expertise to many nonprofit organizations. Her first public service project was 17 years ago, when she hosted the telethon for the Muscular Dystrophy Association, a nonprofit organization that sponsors research for a group of 40 inherited diseases marked by progressive weakness and degeneration of the skeletal, or voluntary, muscles that control movement. MDA is one of Kim's favorite causes. She says, "You can't be involved in something that long without getting to know the people. These are our neighbors and friends. So it's become a big part of my life."

Over the years there have been many community causes that the station has adopted and Kim has given freely of herself and her time. She has served on the board of the Rape Crisis Center for almost 12 years. The Kidney Association, the Heart Association, and the Salvation Army have all benefited from Kim's support. She is also the honorary chairperson of the Pine Tree Society's 24-hour relay, and is on the Board of Directors for the Ronald McDonald House and Camp Sunshine. "You cannot do stories about the problems people are facing without being deeply touched yourself, especially when it involves children," Kim explains.

All the camaraderie and goodwill you see among the news team on Channel 13 is also there when the cameras aren't on. "We're a very close group," says Kim. "We have to be, because when everyone's pushing deadlines, you're literally bumping into each other to get things ready on time. We have to have a lot of flexibility. For the most part, egos just are not part of the picture here. Everyone has a job to do and we all need each other. You can't fake a good attitude. It doesn't work on camera – or off. It helps when everyone likes everyone else on the team. And that goes for the team behind the scenes, too, the ones the public doesn't see. Those of us in front of the camera couldn't be in front of the camera without the behind-the-scenes crew and staff who support us and make us look good. When you co-anchor, you have to anticipate each other's moves and comments."

Anchoring the TV news sounds like a glamorous job, doesn't it? There's nothing glamorous about working 3 PM to midnight, which sometimes happens when someone is away and coworkers have to cover. Contrary to what people might think, a news anchor doesn't just breeze through the door at 5:45 and walk onto the set. "I do a great deal of the writing for our broadcasts. We all share that responsibility with the producers and the reporters. Our team starts putting together a newscast at 2:30 in the morning, monitoring the scanners and reading the newspapers to determine what is going to go on the air. We have a morning meeting with our reporters and our assignment desk people to decide who's going to cover what and who's going to go where with whom. A great many people are involved in the coverage of each day's news. The ultimate decision of what to include in each newscast is made by that show's producer."

One of the givens about news is that it doesn't happen when it's convenient. Like everyone else, Kim has to accommodate her schedule, which is difficult because her first child is three years old. "My career is very important to me," Kim says, "but it's a lot more difficult than I thought it was going to be. Being a working mom is tough, no matter what career you have, but it's particularly difficult in broadcasting because my job doesn't stop when I go home. I can't even go to the grocery store without someone saying, 'Aren't you Kim Block? You don't look the same as you do on TV!' Believe me, I look very different on Saturday morning! And people let me know that! With my job, I can't get away with just putting my hair in a ponytail. I used to get dressed for my work day and then put on one of my husband's big shirts to protect my clothes from the inevitable spills and stains from carrying my son, Miles, in and out of the car. Deciding to work after your first child is an emotional decision. It was a very difficult one for me to make. I have a wonderful daycare situation, which helps a great deal. I count my blessings, believe me."

Becoming a mother made Kim reorder her priorities. She sums it up this way, "When you're single, your career tends to be everything. Then you get married and your life gets divided up a bit differently. Then when children come along, you really rethink your priorities. I'm here to do the very best job I am capable of doing, as always. That hasn't changed. What's changed is that I don't spend all my personal time thinking about my work. Sometimes doing the news gets you very wound up, especially if there's a particularly exciting or moving story that you're reporting. And then I walk into my home and there's this little guy with this huge grin who's so happy to see me. (There's a big guy happy to see me, too!) It's a very wonderful feeling."

Kim's sphere of influence is larger than most women's because she is able to touch so many more lives than someone who is not on TV. "It's important that a journalist and news reporter be unbiased in terms of reporting the news," she explains. "Many of the stories I do are truly one-sided. If a child is in trouble and needs our help, there is only one side to report. It's a very intense responsibility to remember the power of television and the opportunity to influence tremendous numbers of people by the way I relay the news. It's not something I ever take lightly. On the other hand, I think it's important that we use television as a tool to reach out and help each other. That's television at its best and what we hope to achieve at the station.

"Whether it's helping them make a decision on their own or letting them know how they can help another human being, or just presenting solid information, we have tremendous opportunities to make a real difference and that plays a huge role in my life. Sometimes people ask us why the news is always bad. It truly isn't bad all the time. We have goals in mind when we produce the news. We realize it is not just our duty and obligation to report the bad news; there are a lot of positive things that happen around us, too, so we always try to end each broadcast with something positive, something lighter and happier. We call those kickers. Those happy little tidbits at the end of the news are consciously placed there so we can leave people with something positive."

For several years Kim has been the chairperson for the Hearts in Bloom fund-raiser for the American Heart Association. She is also very involved in the Salvation Army's Joy of Sharing. The station has also been strongly supportive of Portland's new Ronald McDonald House. She also recently completed a 60-part series on breast cancer. This was a very ambitious undertaking and one she chose to do. "Sixty parts is a massive project, and producer Maureen O'Brien and I worked very closely on that. We're really pleased with the series. We received so many letters from women who told us they went for a mammogram as a result of watching that series. It made us feel it was worth all the effort." Kim specifically asked to be the Health Watch reporter, because of her interest in medicine. (Her mother was a nurse, her father was a doctor, and Kim studied nursing before switching to broadcast journalism.) "I feel we really are making a difference in people's lives with our Health Watch coverage. People can take an active role in their own health and make a difference, rather than waiting until something goes wrong."

Eighteen years at one station has to be something of a record for a female TV news anchor. Kim Block has reported many stories that touched her deeply, but none so deeply as those involving children. When little Patrick McDonough of Wells needed a bone marrow transplant, she helped get the word out, and that little boy got a second chance at life. When a child in Bath needed a heart transplant, again Kim helped get the word out. All the stories Kim reports for the various telethons touch her compassionate heart. She really can't say no to two causes: health and kids.

Kim has also pulled some really fun assignments in her career. She went to Falmouth, England, to cover the arrival of Bill Dunlop, the man from Falmouth, Maine, who set the world record for sailing solo across the Atlantic. She also covered George Bush's inauguration in Washington, D.C. "To be doing the news in Washington D.C. (where I grew up) was really fun, kind of a dream come true for me. I'll probably never live there again, because my home is here now, but it was a lot of fun to work there on that special assignment. It was a real highlight for me."

Kim's message to women is simple: "Give something back, because you can make a difference in people's lives. Each of us has within ourselves the power to make a difference. There is no greater feeling than knowing that you have helped your community, your friends, your family, even a stranger. I have a unique opportunity to do this because of my career in broadcasting. Community service is a huge part of my job. I don't think I realized that when I slid off those phone books at my audition! I make several public appearances each month for different charities, and I meet so many wonderful people who are out there quietly doing things to help others. It's humbling and at the same time there's a certain amount of responsibility that comes with being a public person. Everyone here at the station has opportunities to be involved in community projects, and the majority of them do get involved and give of themselves. This is not just a job; it's a way of life."

It's for that attitude that we include Kim Block in this book – not Kim Block the TV personality, but Kim Block, the woman, who gives so much of herself and her time to help other people live a better, fuller life.

Margaret Chase Smith

Serving Her Country with Courage, Compassion and Common Sense

At first glance, they look like flags. But from what countries? Then the realization dawns: these are academic hoods – 93 of them – granted to a remarkable woman in recognition of her extraordinary life and career in public service. U.S. Senator Margaret Chase Smith has received 95 honorary degrees in all: the first was a Masters from Colby College and the last was a Doctorate from the same institution. The hoods hang around the periphery of the foyer in the Margaret Chase Smith Library in Skowhegan, Maine, their colorful and graceful folds presiding over the mementos and memorabilia of 32 years of service to her country.

Born in Skowhegan, Maine, in 1897, Margaret Chase briefly taught school, worked for the Skowhegan newspaper and served as an executive with a textile firm before marrying Clyde H. Smith in 1930. He was 57 to her 32, and was a respected politician who held numerous local and state offices. When he was elected to Congress in 1936, Margaret moved to Washington with him and served as his secretary until his death from a heart attack in 1940. She had to meet impossible deadlines in order to do it, but she ran in a special election in order to finish her husband's term in the U.S. House of Representatives. She won, and went on to be the first woman to be elected to both houses of Congress. She never had children, nor did she remarry. Instead, she gave her life to championing individual rights and serving the people of Maine, and the nation.

"The turning point in my career was when I decided to run for Senator," she reminisces. "When I became a member of the Senate in January 1949, no one challenged the sanctity of the seniority system. Nor did anyone propose that any special consideration be given to the only woman in the Senate. Consequently, I drew the lowest ranking Senate assignments. Not until I had served four years in the Senate did I receive a major committee assignment."

Never one to dodge an issue, Margaret spoke out for what she believed was best for her constituents and for the Nation. She established her reputation early as a woman of ability and great conviction. The political climate in Washington at that time was filled with cold war issues and fear of nuclear war. As she went about her duties in Washington, she observed an unsettling situation resulting from the accusations of Senator Joe McCarthy aimed at colleagues he deemed un-American. Senator Smith became increasingly alarmed at Senator Joe McCarthy's tendency to see as a communist anyone who disagreed with him, producing fear in even the most stalwart men in the Senate. Accusation followed accusation as McCarthy lashed out at anyone he perceived as a threat. Margaret watched as the charged atmosphere in the Senate prevented the work they had been elected to do from getting done.

"I was concerned because he did not produce evidence to back up his serious charges against people. Week after week went by with charge after charge by Joe McCarthy which remained unproved. My doubts increased. Finally I became convinced that he simply was not going to come up with any proof to substantiate his charges. McCarthy had created an atmosphere of such political fear that people were not only afraid to talk, but they were afraid of whom they might be seen with. In those days freshman Senators were to be seen and not heard. The Senate was paralyzed with fear. The political risk of taking issue with him was too great a hazard to the political security of Senators."

One woman decided to speak her conscience. On June 1, 1950, Margaret Chase Smith stood on the floor of the United States Senate and delivered what became known as her *Declaration of Conscience* speech. The issues may be different, but the challenge to our elected officials is just as apropos today as it was 45 years ago. "I think it is high time for the United States Senate and its members to do some soul-searching – for us to weigh our consciences – on the manner in which we are performing our duty to the people of America – on the manner in which we are using or abusing our individual powers and privileges."

Her speech focused attention not only on the problem, but also on the woman Senator from Maine. From speculation on her potential future as a Vice President to her selection as one of the *Ten Best Tailored Women of the World*, Margaret Chase Smith was in the spotlight. Her fellow Senators praised her privately, but when she asked one why he didn't speak out as she had, he replied, "Margaret! That would be political suicide!" Suicidal or not, Margaret could not just sit by and watch what was happening. Her honesty, her integrity, and her dedication to serving the American people, propelled her to her feet that day in the Senate, and her impassioned delivery spoke to the conscience of nearly everyone in the room.

What strength of character! It was that strength that got her through the next years of retaliation aimed at defeating her politically. McCarthy himself came to Maine to campaign against her by holding up her opponent as someone the people of Maine should send to Washington. At a press conference, McCarthy asked if there was anyone stronger politically with the people of Maine than Senator Smith. He brightened up and a smile covered his face when one reporter finally said, "Yes. There is one who is stronger with Maine people than Margaret Smith." With eager anticipation, Joe [McCarthy] asked, "Who?" Solemnly and slowly the reporter replied, "Almighty God." And that was the end of that. Margaret won the election 5 to 1, and effectively broke the stranglehold McCarthyism had on the Senate.

"In my service in the U.S. House of Representatives," Margaret remembers, "I was identified more with WAVE (Women Accepted for Volunteer Emergency Service — Navy) legislation. It left the impression, I'm afraid, that I was a feminist concentrating on legislation for women. And if there is any one thing I have attempted to avoid, it is being a feminist. I definitely resent being called a feminist."

In spite of that statement, Representative Smith most definitely believed, however, in equality for women. She felt that if there were a need for women in the armed services after the war, they should be granted regular status, as well as reserve status. If there were no need, they shouldn't be kept on active duty. "I challenged the services to prove that they needed the women in specific jobs before I would support legislation to give them peacetime status." The women got their permanent Regular status because one woman had refused to give up in the face of overwhelming odds against her.

In 1969, in a speech to the Business and Professional Women's Club in Washington, Margaret put the responsibility for women's status in society squarely on women's shoulders. "It took women years and years and years of a very hard struggle to achieve economic security and freedom. But it did not take such a hard struggle to have the physical and biological security and freedom that the pill has so suddenly and explosively brought...such power should be very carefully exercised lest it ultimately be the self-destruction of woman and her rightful and responsible place in civilization rather than man-kind." The speech received a very chilly reception. (This was the 1940s, remember.) Margaret was warning that the dignity of women was in jeopardy unless women continued to earn it, and unless they exercised their earned – and their unearned – power with great care and responsibility.

By the 1960s, speculation had persisted for several years about putting Senator Smith's name on the national ticket as Vice President. Unexpectedly her name was being suggested for the Presidential slot and she received a significant volume of mail from all over the country urging her to seek the nomination. On December 1, 1963, the editor of the San Diego Union wrote: "If Mrs. Smith announces she will enter the New Hampshire primary in March, her presence would have to be taken seriously...Whether the country or either party is ready for a woman on the presidential ticket remains to be seen. But Mrs. Smith will have her say. And just the possibility that she may run has advanced the cause of women candidates, perhaps more than most of their male opponents realize."

At the Women's National Press Club luncheon on January 27, 1964, Margaret gave a masterful speech in which she enumerated many reasons people had given both for and against her running for President. She had the audience on the edge of their seats as she concluded, "As

174

gratifying as are the reasons advanced urging me to run, I find the reasons advanced against my running to be far more impelling....So because of these very impelling reasons against my running, I have decided that I shall enter the New Hampshire Presidential preferential primary and the Illinois primary. For I accept the reasons advanced against my running as challenges...I welcome the challenges and I look forward to the test."

The audience roared with delight, and Margaret Chase Smith had chalked up another first for her record. As with everything else in her life, Senator Smith dove into the race for the presidential nomination with gusto. She hit the campaign trail at six-thirty that first morning at Pittsburg, New Hampshire, near the Canadian border. The first two voters she approached were loading pulpwood on a truck at the roadside. When she stopped at the general store, the temperature was 28 degrees below zero.

At the Republican National Convention in July of 1964 she had only 16 delegates pledged to her, but her name was placed in nomination for the Presidency of the United States by Senator George Aiken of Vermont – the first woman to be so honored. The editor of the New Bern, North Carolina, *Mirror* wrote of the significance of Senator Smith's candidacy: "...it gave millions of Americans a televised glimpse of one of this country's great public servants...[who]...managed to retain the graciousness and charm that has characterized not only her personal life but her career in Congress."

Twenty years to the day from her first *Declaration of Conscience*, Margaret addressed her colleagues in the U.S. Senate. She saw symptoms of another national illness taking hold. "The disease this time was unlimited and crass pragmatism – the creed that the end justifies the means...and get whatever you can, regardless of how you do it." She concluded her second *Declaration of Conscience* with this challenge:

"It is time that the great center of our people, those who reject the violence and unreasonableness of both the extreme right and the extreme left, searched their consciences, mustered their moral and physical courage, shed their intimidated silence, and declared their consciences.

"It is time that with dignity, firmness and friendliness, they reason with, rather than capitulate to, the extremists on both sides – at all levels – and caution that their patience ends at the border of violence and anarchy that threatens our American democracy."

One of Margaret Chase Smith's favorite sayings is "Give to the world the best you have and the best will come back to you." In her 97 years she has done just that: given her best effort, whatever the task before her. Throughout her long and unusual career in government, Senator Smith stood her ground, insisted on her rights as a Senator, refused to be discriminated against, refused special treatment just because she was a woman, and voted her conscience. Smeared, maligned, lied about and vilified, she never gave in. She defended herself with the truth and her impeccable record. She always paid her own way, never accepting a campaign contribution, except one. That was a jar of pennies a group of school children had collected and presented to her to help with campaign expenses. That one touched her so deeply, she kept it and gave it a place of honor.

Author's Note: Shortly after this story appeared in The Maine Woman magazine, Margaret Chase Smith died in her home in Skowhegan on June 16, 1995. The world had given back to her over 270 honors and awards, as well as the 95 honorary degrees. She is still loved and respected by Mainers, young and old, who know how she lived her life and how she served her people. She was a gracious, elegant and eloquent example of what one woman can do when her life is lived in service to others.

Her memorial service was a celebration of her life, attended by hundreds, including some of this country's greatest leaders who had served with her, as well as by little school children from down the street who had visited with her at her home, or in the course of daily life in Skowhegan had sat in the booth next to hers at the local restaurant. At the end of the service, the Navy Band (flown in from Washington, D.C.) swung into a triumphant rendition of one of Margaret's favorites, Peg 'o My Heart, that the audience sang with gusto – and tears – giving Margaret a send-off she would have reveled in. The following article appeared in the issue of The Maine Woman following her death.

Just Margaret

I hang up the phone. I have goose bumps. "We're waiting for a call," he said. "Tell her I called?" I asked. "I will. Thanks, Alice." Something is not right. I sense it. It is 4.42 P.M. on Memorial Day, Monday, May 29ᵗʰ. I turn on the TV as I start dinner preparations and hear the news reporter saying, "Margaret Chase Smith died at 4:40 P.M. today in her Skowhegan home." I put down the pot I am holding. 4:40 P.M. was the exact minute I had dialed the Senator's home to tell her companion, Sister Joyce Mahany, that we were praying for the Senator and for her, too, in this difficult situation. Watching someone you love lie there day after day in a coma is emotionally and physically draining and my heart went out to Sister Joyce, Greg Gallant, the staff and the Senator's family and friends.

I remember the day I first called the Senator's home to tell her I wanted to honor her by putting her on the cover of The Maine Woman. Sister Joyce thought the Senator would be pleased, and she was. "The Lady from Maine" graced the cover of our March issue. So many people were deeply touched by her words and her character, but no one was touched more deeply than I.

My husband and I delivered a dozen long-stemmed red roses to the Senator along with copies of her issue of The Maine Woman on March 5th. She was not up, but she wanted to see us. Sister Joyce greeted us at the reception desk with, "That's a cute dog in your car." I replied automatically, "That's Duffee, my Westie. He loves everyone." Sister Joyce said, "The Senator likes dogs." "That's nice," I said, not catching on. Sister Joyce tried again, "But the Senator really loves dogs." I woke up. "Oooooo-kay. I'll go get the dog!" The Senator was 100% there as she received us. There was a sparkle in her blue eyes as we talked. Even at 97, she didn't miss a beat. As she thanked me for honoring her in this way, she reached up and took my hand – and she didn't let go until we left, 45 minutes and a half-dozen photos later.

At one point I suggested we should leave so she wouldn't get overtired. "I don't get tired!" she said emphatically. I looked up at Sister Joyce whose wink said otherwise. I said, "Well then, Senator, I'll confess. I'm the one who's exhausted. I need to go home!' Gracious as always, she said, "Of course. But I wish you'd stay." Oh, how I wanted to! I could think of nothing more wonderful than spending hour after hour sitting beside this paragon of public service and gleaning any scrap of wisdom she cared to bestow. I wanted to ask her a million things: How did she think America was doing? Did she think our educational system really prepared kids for life? What was her favorite memory of life in Washington? Would she teach me to play bridge? But there wasn't time.

"I really have to go home, Senator," I said as I squeezed her hand. Then inspiration struck. "Do you like lemon meringue pie?" I asked her. "Who doesn't?" came the strong reply without a second's hesitation. We all laughed, including the Senator. "If you'll let me go now, I promise to make you a lemon meringue pie and come back to visit," I offered. "I'll look forward to that," she agreed. I picked Duffee up in my arms and held him so she could pat him. He was his usual personable self. Another conquest. Then he looked up at me as if to say, "Does this make me First Dog of Maine?"

Three weeks later, I returned to the house on the hill in Skowhegan with two made-from-scratch lemon meringue pies and an armload of daffodils. The Senator and I shared a short visit, as Duffee lay at her feet. Prompt as always, two days later, I received this personal thank you. "How very kind you were to return with the delicious lemon meringue pies which I have shared with the staff and visiting students from Michigan and Florida, selfishly keeping plenty for myself. It was good seeing you again. With best wishes, as always, and many thanks. Sincerely, Margaret."

Just "Margaret." For me, that says it all.

I didn't know you long enough, Margaret Chase Smith, and I miss you already.

Maribeth Vander Weele

Telling It As It Is
to Bring Accountability to the Chicago School System

It's no surprise that Maribeth Vander Weele had a career in journalism. As a child she pretended to be a newspaper reporter. She and her mother would spend hours by the fireplace, reading and talking about what they had read. Because her dad was a volunteer firefighter, Maribeth Vander Weele and her six brothers and sisters would all pile into the station wagon and follow him to the where the action was. At 16 she was a stringer for the local paper. "I grew up with a built-in lust for being on the front lines of breaking news," she laughs, "so there was never any question of what career I would choose!"

Several factors set Maribeth's feet on the particular path her journalism career followed. "My older sister was a child of the 60s and she took me to some of the milder protests that were so prevalent then, teaching me at an early age to look at government with an analytical and critical eye. During a summer internship at the City News Bureau of Chicago, a wire service serving the major news media in the area, I learned the hard facts of life in the inner city. I was appalled at the conditions people were living in and vowed that someday I would do something to help. Also while I was in college, I served an internship for the Chicago Sun Times in Washington D.C. That is where I learned to use computers and the art of record analysis to produce news stories – a method I still use. After college, I went to work for a small south suburban newspaper in Chicago Heights, a very Mafia-influenced area. You do everything at a small newspaper. I had general assignments, and my beat was government and crime. When I moved to the next job, I was again asked to cover government, and I got an entire education in government spending. Again, I vowed to use my career to someday make a difference. I believe all these experiences prepared me for what I am doing today. Nothing is ever wasted, even if we cannot see the purpose in an experience when we are going through it."

Maribeth gained a reputation for incisive, accurate reporting of the facts, with hard-hitting conclusions. Her stories had the ring of truth that nobody could deny. She excelled as a documents reporter, using what she discovered in public documents and records of what people themselves had actually said, instead of second-hand reporting of what had been said.

Then, in 1990, she went to work for the Chicago Sun Times, assigned to education, specifically the Chicago public schools — a job no one else on the paper wanted. One of her first invitations was from a local school council member to visit one of the schools. What had once been a grand old building complete with a greenhouse and with walls four to five feet thick, had been allowed to deteriorate to an appalling condition. The roof had been leaking for over twenty years. Big chunks of plaster were missing from the ceiling; others were hanging there, ready to fall on unsuspecting heads. Not just drips, but waterfalls were streaming down the sides of classroom walls. Daylight was visible through the ceiling of the teachers' washroom. Of course, materials were full of lead and asbestos. It was an outrageous situation, and Maribeth's initial story made the front page of the Chicago Sun Times, launching a lengthy series appropriately called Schools in Ruins, which she co-authored. The stories were incredible, but the conditions were worse. Maribeth asked the question that had only one answer: How can children learn anything under these deplorable conditions?

Using her technique of investigative and documented reporting,

Maribeth told the public that there had been no preventive maintenance because the Director of Facilities for the Chicago Schools claimed there had been no money to repair the buildings. Criminal investigators proved he had been taking hundreds of thousands in bribes from contractors for work that had been paid for, but had never been done. There were outrageous overcharges such as a hundred dollars for a 70-cent wall switch. The corruption was so deeply entrenched, that the school system had spent millions of dollars, and had little to show for it.

Maribeth explains, "The extent of the corruption was truly astonishing, especially in the light of how needy our children were. The money slated for repairs and building maintenance to keep our children safe in our school buildings was lining the pockets of the dishonest contractors. We targeted this area in our reporting and brought a lot of the corruption to light. The Director of Facilities was indicted. It was unconscionable that he could go to sleep at night knowing that Chicago's school children were suffering. It was also unconscionable that the School Board let it happen. I produced a steady stream of investigations about the problem, but even with the convictions and imprisonments, I still felt that no one listened, because things weren't turning around. My reporting did not produce massive protests, and that made me feel discouraged, but I wouldn't give up, even though it seemed hopeless. Everyone knows that education is the key to so much, including the building of a vibrant city. It stunned me that there was nothing happening to change things."

After five frustrating years, Maribeth decided to put her findings into book form and challenge the decision-makers in Illinois – the legislators. This was not part of her job at the paper, so she wrote from 6 P.M. to midnight, as well as every Saturday and Sunday. She hoped that if she could pull all the facts she had uncovered together in one place, it would effect change. The book didn't just identify problems in the school system; it suggested possible solutions. Writing the book proved to be the right thing to do. Illinois' Lieutenant Governor sent a copy of the book to every state legislator. Members of the state's Education Committee (who lived many miles from Chicago) now knew the story of how the taxes were being spent, and misspent.

One result was that the legislature said enough was enough, and placed the management of the entire school system under Mayor Richard

Daley. Prior to this, he had only had limited control, because school board members were nominated through a grass roots nominating commission. Gery Chico was appointed as president of the board, Paul Vallas, Revenue Director for the city, was selected as the chief executive officer of the school system and he appointed Maribeth as part of the management team whose mission it was to reshape the schools. That was in 1995, and the results have been incredible. Not only have they exceeded the team's hopes, they are making news.

One of the first things the new team did was put into effect some of the solutions Maribeth had suggested for key problem areas identified in her book. For example, inner city Chicago's population is usually less moneyed, so they tend to be more transient and move often. In the school system, that translated into thousands of kids sitting in study halls with no teacher until October, because, not knowing exactly how many kids they would have, they didn't hire the teachers until after the enrollment took place in September. The best teachers usually can't wait around, so they would take firm offers from elsewhere. The situation had a terrible effect on the education of the kids. Vallas' team instituted an early enrollment procedure where the students enroll by June, before school is on summer break. This has made a dramatic improvement and has also allowed the system to recruit well-qualified teachers. There had been a lot of strikes and instability, with no one ever knowing for sure if the schools were going to open on schedule. The team also cut over a billion dollars from the budget, vastly improving the system in the process, and enabling us to save over 100 million dollars over four years.

"Another problem," Maribeth explains, "was that more than 10,000 kids were arrested a year, but less than a handful would be expelled. The gangs were in control. In addition to starting a truancy hotline, which was responsible for getting more than 2000 children back into school in the first eight months it was in operation, the team also set a very strong discipline policy, good for teachers and students alike. It's a zero-tolerance policy: no drugs and no guns in the school or you will be expelled and sent to an alternative school for violent youth. The past administration had eliminated alternative schools, which sent a strong negative message. But the safety of our children and staff was of paramount importance. It's vital for kids to learn that in life, every action has a consequence.

"Teacher accountability is of vital importance to any school system. The school district now has a teacher accountability unit which gives principals educational and legal support to work with their poorly-performing teachers. This accountability program remediates them to be better teachers, or provides a way of removing them from the classroom. Another problem was that the local school councils had been pressuring school principals to hire council members' relatives, no matter what type of teaching credentials they possessed. The team was instrumental in passing an ethics ordinance to prohibit nepotism, and was also able to institute a financial accountability program for schools that were not handling their money properly.

"I had included a chapter in my book on social promotion. Kids who had never turned in an assignment or rarely attended school were being sent to the next grade. This sent a message that they never need perform, and encouraged a culture of low expectations. Of the 425,000 students in the system, every year 1/3 were graduating already two years behind the national average. Our average freshman had a 6ᵗʰ grade reading score. And that didn't even count the 50% who had dropped out! Even though the dropout rate is now down to slightly less than 50%, it's still true that less than half of every kindergarten class doesn't make it to high school graduation. The school board had a policy that you could not hold a child back more than once in elementary school. Paul Vallas instituted a program that allows a child to be held back if necessary in 3rd, 6th, 8th and 9th grades or the child will go to mandatory summer school in order not to be retained. The summer school program has been enormously successful. The message to the kids is that they have to meet standards in order to move forward.

"Nothing hurts a child's self esteem more than entering the work world or applying for college unprepared. It's a shock for ill-prepared graduates to apply for a job and discover their skills are inadequate. Some had been honor students and assumed that they were competitive with other schools' graduates. Self esteem emanates partly from accomplishment, and our system was promoting self esteem at the expense of achievement or accomplishment. This damaging practice has been reversed. Test scores have steadily gone up. Attendance is up.

Enrollment is up. Drop-outs are down; 80% of the kids in this year's summer school will be promoted to the next grade after intensive math and English instruction.

"When I first unearthed the educational disaster that was the Chicago school system while working at the Chicago Sun Times, I had asked how it could be possible for a child to go through 12 years of education and graduate not knowing how to read? Some of our college prep kids were reading at 2nd and 3rd grade levels. Over 50% of our Chicago high schools scored in the bottom 1% of the nation on the American College Testing Exam. We needed to do better for Chicago's kids. That became my mission.

"I didn't implement all these things personally," Maribeth says, "but the book pinpointed the problem areas and was the catalyst for change. Finally, things began to happen to correct the incredible mismanagement of the school system! And we are all the winners, especially the children. Other cities are looking at what we're doing and are beginning to copy our programs. My dream is to see these reforms go nationwide!"

The old saying is still very much true: One person can make a difference. Tens of thousands of school children in Chicago Schools will have a better chance in life because one investigative reporter didn't quit until the situation began to change for the better. Yet, Maribeth Vander Weele does not take credit for the remarkable changes in the Chicago Schools. "It was very much a team effort," she says. "I just pulled all the facts together in my book and gave it to the people who could effect change. It's been my privilege to be a part of the process of getting the school system back on track. My advice to women? Never compromise your conscience. Walk with courage."

Linda Woodard

Teaching Kids to Color Their World Green

There's a cormorant in her bathtub and a bat in the box under her arm. Unusual? Not for Linda Woodard! She is Director of the Scarborough Marsh Nature Center for Maine Audubon Society. She also coordinates all the volunteers for Audubon's walk program and facilitates all the teacher workshops, as well as managing the Teacher Resource Center. "It excites me to interact with people," Linda explains.

"I think teaching and learning are two sides of the same coin. If you're a good teacher, you're also a learner. I especially love working with children because they have this sense of awe about them when they learn something new and that's really exciting to me."

What instilled a love of nature in Linda? "My parents took me camping when I was six months old!" she laughs. "So I learned my love of nature from them. It's just always been a big part of my life. I used to get the Ranger Rick magazine every month as I was growing up. My father is a college professor and my mother is an elementary school teacher, and they taught me well. They're very supportive. My mother taught me to think. I learned to ask why. And she always told me why."

With that kind of nurturing, it was a natural for Linda to pursue

185

a career as an animal medical technologist. After graduation, she worked for a veterinarian for a couple of years, and then discovered she was allergic to some animals, especially cats, which she adores! Obviously, she had to make a change in careers, so she went back to school and earned her bachelors degree in biology. "I got a job doing cellular research in a lab – with the doors shut!" she grins. "Being inside all the time was really hard for me, even though I really liked the research process."

She found the answer to her frustration in the newspaper: an ad for two volunteers for Maine Audubon at Scarborough Marsh. Linda and her friend, Richard Duddy, applied and started volunteering. Thirteen years later, they're still volunteering together. Linda shares her life with two special pets, a horse named Maybe that she saved from the auction block, and Zeus, a gentle German Shepherd who accompanies her almost everywhere.

Linda works for the Maine Audubon Society where environmental education is one of the major goals of Maine Audubon and Linda is committed to introducing Mainers to their own flora and fauna. She explains, "The objectives of the nature studies programs are to arouse awareness, provide information, increase appreciation, stimulate concern and motivate to action. One of the methods we use is our four-season ecology walks. Children are better at noticing things than adults, but they still need help in knowing what to look for. It's really fun to see them light up all of a sudden when they grasp the concepts. We keep the groups small on purpose, 10 participants per guide, and spend an hour outside and then a half hour inside. We talk about the animal mounts in our resource center and how the animals adapt to different seasons. Outside, we look at the plants and animals and how they adapt to the seasons. We start by looking for signs of animals: scratchings on the trees, a half-eaten acorn or apple, or tracks. We also go to the Scarborough Marsh for walks in the summer, which is open to the public from June to September. At the Marsh we get a lot of people who just stumble across us on their way to the beach or someplace else, and it's fun for us when they don't know anything about nature. One of our prime objectives is to evoke that emotional response which results in a bond with nature. Then they'll want to know more. If someone tells me they didn't see anything, I take them back outside and point out a few things. Then they say, Wow! I can't

"We try to get people excited about nature and how we're a part of the cycle. What we want to get across is their personal connection with nature. Then they will want to know more and may become a nature advocate on a governmental level. We want them to think of themselves as part of nature, a part of the process, a part of the food chain. We have to be mindful of what we're doing in nature, and what our role is. We'll have the children act out the food chain. For example, one will be a small fish, the next one will be a larger fish, the next will be a great blue heron. The next would be a fox who would eat the heron. This helps children see what happens if we eliminate one link in the chain. They really get the picture. When we see a kill, we use it to illustrate the food chain. We don't tell them it's right or wrong to eat meat or fish, for example. We just make them aware of where their food comes from and let them decide. We teach them about habitats and discuss how to protect them. We don't just look at the species, but the habitat. It's very important to think about recycling and solid wastes and what we're consuming and how we're replacing those resources. Right now a lot of us are on a linear path; we consume and consume and consume. We have to think about making it a cycle instead."

Linda also facilitates a lot of teacher workshops and runs the Teacher Resource Center. Showing teachers how to educate the children is a big part of Linda's work, and a part she absolutely loves. "The key now is integrated teaching," she enthuses. "Not just having science and math and English, but integrating it all into the whole picture. We show them how to use their school grounds as a teaching tool. I've gone into some schools in cities where they don't have any trees or ponds or much to work with to illustrate nature on the property. So I've shown them how to use puddles. It's amazing what you can learn from Puddle Biology!

"One of my favorite stories is from a teacher workshop with a group of city teachers, one of whom taught emotionally disturbed students. For whatever the reasons, the school administration didn't want her to take the students outside. I spent a lot of time with her, giving her ideas she could use, and after the workshop, I called her to see how things were going. She was so committed to exposing these kids to nature, that she went to the school committee and really pushed to get the kids outside. She told me she got permission to take them on a hike up Bradbury Mountain in the fall.

"She described it to me this way: One particularly difficult student stood on top of the mountain and looked out at the fall foliage and the beauty of nature spread out around him. He was very close to tears. He looked up at me and said, 'Is this heaven?' I didn't have any problems with him after that. And it's all because of you, Linda. I was really touched.

"It means a lot to me to know that I've been able to make even a small difference in someone's life because I know the joy that being outdoors brings. I can have a bad day once in a while, but then I go outside for a walk and I get my perspective back. I wonder how many people drive by a tree with beautiful leaves and birds' nests and squirrels doing acrobatics above their heads and they don't even notice the tree! They're missing so much! Those are the people I want to reach."

In her spare time, Linda is outdoors as much as possible, often volunteering at Audubon-sponsored events when she is off-duty. Sometimes she gets calls at home about injured birds or animals that someone has found. Because of her veterinary medicine background, she has been able to take care of various injured wildlife. She works with the Center for Wildlife out of York, Maine, a rehabilitative facility with huge flight cages. Because of the recent rabies scare, the state has told a lot of rehabbers not to take in sick or injured mammals. By the time they get the animal, it's usually so sick they can't save it.

"People mean well, but they just don't know what they're doing," Linda explains. "It's actually against the law to possess a bird's nest or a bird's feather, except for house sparrows, starlings and pigeons. The reason is enforcement. Some people have killed the birds just to get a feather. Even taking in a baby bird is against the law. One woman called me and said she'd found a baby bird and had fed it milk. It died. So we have trained rehabilitators. I carry a rehab permit, so I'm allowed to have bird feathers."

Linda also volunteers at Baxter School for the Deaf and is learning sign language so she can teach the kids about nature. "Those kids are wonderful," she says. "They appreciate so much what you do for them. They can't hear the birds. They have to learn what the habitat is like, then look for them."

1996 was the 25th anniversary at the Scarborough Marsh facility. In October devastating floods destroyed the parking lot and undermined the buildings. "We had to rip up the rugs and tear out the wall boards and insulation due to water damage." Linda says. "Even though I was deeply concerned about getting the Center up and running again, as always has been the case here, the volunteers rallied and went to work. Then on Christmas Eve, I got a call that the Center had been vandalized. My friend, Richard Duddy, and I spent the afternoon boarding up the broken windows, but we ran out of plywood and couldn't get more due to the holiday, and more were broken in the next few days. Volunteers helped, but a few days later, it was vandalized again. They didn't steal anything, but broke every glass surface, including our glass display cases and a 75 gallon fish tank.

"I contacted the media and public response was amazing. Our story was on the news at 6:10, and by 6:25, I had a pledge for a new fish tank. By the next morning, someone donated a glass display case. Volunteers came from everywhere! I went from being so totally demoralized to being awed at the caring response. When spring came and it was time to start fixing up the Center, we had several contractors and individuals donate several thousand dollars worth of time and equipment. Two local boy scout troops and a sorority from the local university also pitched in. Many volunteers helped get the Center back together.

"In June we had a 25th anniversary celebration. It was a very special day because not only were we celebrating 25 years of nature programs at the Marsh, but we had survived a major flood and vandalism. We not only brought the Center back to its original condition, but it is much better, with a new discovery room, displays and a picnic table. I never worked as hard, nor have I ever felt such a feeling of satisfaction and elation in my work as I did when I watched the Center come back to life.

"Working with nature and kids gives me hope for the future. Sometimes I get bogged down and discouraged when I hear some of the ways we are squandering and abusing our natural resources with no thought of what will be left for the next generation. Sometimes I don't even want to listen to the news or read the paper. But then I remember that little girl on the nature walk whose eyes lit up when she realized she was a part of the food chain, or that elementary school teacher at the in-service workshop who got really excited about teaching her asphalt-bound city school kids about the life in a puddle of rain water. And I realize that what I'm doing with my life is a part of the life-chain, and that I have a commission to fulfill. Then my perspective returns and I get excited all over again!"

Linda is serving as a mentor for a program called Girls and Women Seizing Science Together in one of the local middle schools. With her usual enthusiasm bubbling over, she is excited about this opportunity to spend her free time teaching people about nature. "What I do is not just my job; it's a way of life! If I could talk to parents, I'd encourage them to develop an affinity with nature: Get out and do some exploring. Learn to really look at the world around you – in detail. Keep an open mind and be ready to learn right along with your children. Children need to hear both sides of environmental issues. And then look at each side critically. Let your children make up their minds from the facts. Watch the news with your kids and discuss it with them. Especially as it relates to nature. It's exciting to see a child get turned on to nature and ecology. Don't miss out on this experience with your children."

D.J. Stanhope

Offering Help, Healing and A Home to Those in Recovery

If you're single, female, homeless, and working toward recovery, there is only one place available to you in Portland, Maine. Faith House is the place to go, and D.J. Stanhope is the woman to see. How D.J. became the executive director of both Faith and Friendship Houses is a fascinating story.

"My dad was in the military" D.J. reminisces, "and was always being sent overseas. Having him gone so much fostered insecurity in certain areas of my life. My mom is an incredibly gifted woman, and she sacrificed all her own goals to be a terrific mother to the three of us kids. Because we moved around constantly, I got used to becoming whatever I had to become in order to make friends. It was my own insecurity and wanting to belong that led me to begin using drugs and alcohol in high school. I didn't like myself, and had a lot of fears. Never living two years in the same place was difficult, to say the least, and got more difficult as I got older. I was always having to pull up stakes and start over again someplace new."

It's understandable that D.J., like so many young people, slipped into alcohol and drug addiction. Now, she believes that it was all part of some master plan for her life. "I was incredibly liberal, incredibly idealistic, without having any real experience in the world," she reflects. "Until ten years ago," she explains, "my life just drifted from one thing –

and from one place – to another. I didn't know who I was; my addictions were in control. That was the darkest period of my life. I finally realized I needed help and my parents flew me home. I had my cat and $35 in my pocket, and that was all. I knew I had a problem, but didn't call it what it was – an addiction to drugs and alcohol.

"I went to work in the family business, but my personal life didn't improve. Then I met the man of my dreams and we were engaged. I thought he was everything I wanted. But the day came when I realized I was putting the alcohol before the relationship, and that was the turning point in my thinking. I saw myself at the edge of an abyss and I was utterly terrified. That realization was an immediate epiphany. I knew I was at a crossroads, and that I had a choice to make right then. I was literally killing myself with the drinking, the drugging and the smoking. After the longest 15 minutes of my life, I walked across the room, and picked up the phone book to look for help. With that call for help, my life did a 180-degree turnaround. About two and a half months later, I was in a car accident. I couldn't do anything. I was out of work for four months. It gave me time to get my life back in order. I went back to basics, and even began going back to church.

"Over the next year, I worked very hard to discover who I was. My fiancé and I postponed our marriage, and we both did a lot of work on discovering who we each really were. Our marriage never happened. (He married in 1994, and I was his best man!) I'm very happy for him, and for me, too, because I know that was the way it was supposed to be."

Looking back, D.J. says she realizes now that everything she went through was preparation for her work. She immersed herself in service work in the community, and got a job that allowed her the schedule to concentrate on her priorities. One of the close friends D.J. made at her church was Louise Montgomery, the founder of Faith and Friendship Houses. In December of 1986 Louise opened Friendship House as a shelter for the homeless in Portland, Maine. At that time there was none. People had to go to the jail and sleep in cots in the gymnasium to get out of the cold. Friendship House accommodates 10 men and Faith House (opened in December of 1991) can house 5 women. Both Faith and Friendship Houses feel like home, not just shelters. "People in recovery need to feel grounded," D.J. explains.

In November of 1992, Louise Montgomery died in a car accident. The Board of Faith and Friendship Houses selected D.J. to be the Executive Director. She was prepared, due to her own life experiences. With her vivacious personality and optimistic, bounce-back attitude, the redheaded bubble of enthusiasm known as D.J. was ready-made for the job.

D.J. explains, "There is no shelter in Portland for homeless single women in recovery other than Faith House. It's for women who are trying to put their lives back together. If someone doesn't qualify for other social agency help, this is the only place available. People who live at Faith and Friendship Houses have to have the *desire* to get their lives back on track. I don't ask anything of anyone who lives here that I wouldn't be willing to do myself. I have been where they are, so I am equipped to help them."

One man at Friendship House, Bill (not his real name) is 51 with a background including college, and a long-term marriage. Bill was a high achiever, in management for years, and is well-spoken. His alcoholism cost him his marriage and a whole lot more. Strangely enough, he had had several periods of sobriety (one over four years), but he always went back to drinking. About a year ago, he quit his management job, and cashed in his 401K retirement plan. Knowing his drinking was out of hand, he still chose to live in a motel room and drink away the thousands of dollars form his retirement fund. One day he was just sitting on his bed, knowing his booze and his money were about to run out, trying to think of ways to end his life. He had decided on a method: slitting his wrists and sitting in a tub of water.

When he went into the bathroom to take his life, he realized with a shock he had lived there three months in that motel room, and he had only a shower. There was no bathtub! At that moment of truth, he hit bottom. Bill went to AA for help, lived at the shelter to detoxify, and then they referred him to Friendship House. Bill says, "What Friendship House has given me is stability, a sense of family and community, and a feeling of self-worth." He's been at Friendship House for about six weeks now, and is waiting for his military records to arrive so he can go to a month-long rehabilitation program at the nearby veterans' hospital. His goal is to go on to a long-term half-way house. D.J. says, "Bill's a wonderful example to others living here. I'm very proud of him and what he's achieved. His goal is to go back to work. He wants to contribute to society again, and I'm confident he'll achieve that. He's got what it takes."

Barbara (not her real name) is another example of how Faith House has helped one person get her life back on track. She was referred to Faith House through a short-term residential rehabilitation program. In the last six years, Barbara had had three years of sobriety, but had spiraled downward. She hit bottom when the state removed her two children from the home and she lost custody. That made her reorder her priorities. People who have never had an addiction problem find it hard to understand how someone could vacillate between sobriety and drunkenness. Barbara says, "You get complacent. You think things are going well and you don't need the AA meetings. I didn't pay attention." She knew that, left to her own devices, she wouldn't make it. She knew she needed the structure of a clean and sober place, like Faith House.

"She's a wonderful person," enthuses D.J. "For her, Faith House has represented a real haven of safety, where she had to learn to get along with others. Faith and Friendship Houses are considered transitional shelters, for the ones who might hit the street between detoxification and the half-way houses. At other shelters, there are still people who use drugs and alcohol and it's hard for someone new in recovery to be around them. There are waiting lists for the long-term half-way houses. Faith and Friendship Houses are the in-between havens for these men and women who are trying to put their lives back together. Some people in recovery need this interim step. When people are 10 days out of detox, they are at the greatest risk for losing their sobriety. It's a very crucial time."

There is no set time that a person can stay at Faith House or Friendship House; however, they must be working toward a goal. D.J. is there to help however she can. "I have regular meetings with the residents. We set goals together – small goals and big goals. We work very hard with our individual guests to help them in taking the next steps in the recovery process so they can move on after they leave here. Each guest is individual and so is his or her recovery. Just as important as setting goals is evaluating the progress each guest has made in achieving those goals. You can't measure progress if you don't know how far you've come. We help our guests assess how they are spending their time – how much time they are spending on their personal relationships, on their emotional and

194

spiritual lives, on achieving their goals. I try to be as transparent as possible to the guests here. They see me when I screw up. I've even had to go across town to apologize to someone! I am also just another person making her own journey."

Update: In September, 1995, D.J. felt that her commission to carry on the work of Louise Montgomery had been fulfilled and it was time for her to move on to other arenas of service. She had offers to work in Central America and Eastern Europe, but the one she accepted was an opportunity to teach with an organization in South Korea. "The most compelling reason for accepting this assignment was my wish to retrace some of my father's steps. (He had served two tours in Korea and two in Vietnam and had been separated from us during these times.) Another influence on my decision was my desire to be changed by my experience, and I was pretty sure that living in the Orient would do that! I felt strongly that there was something I was to do or learn in Asia.

"I spent one year working as an English teacher for an institute in Suwon (a city of 800,000 about 35 miles south of Seoul, Korea)," D.J. says. "I was assigned classes ranging from preschoolers to executives, some taught on site in the schools and factories. Four days a week, I traveled 25 miles through rice paddies and over mountains where elderly men wearing traditional Korean clothing played cards and women walked with great bundles on their heads. In contrast, on my way to church in Seoul I passed beautiful women wearing the most fashionable clothing, talking into cellphones as they walked along boulevards intersecting with ancient winding alleys crowded with merchants and farmers displaying their wares on mats. It's a fascinating country!"

When she felt homesick, D.J. visited the USO at Camp Casey, Korea. The mission of USO is to provide a home away from home to the active duty military stationed abroad as well as to promote good relations between members of the Armed Forces and the host country. When a position with the USO became available, she applied and in June, 1997, she became the Deputy Director of Camp Casey and Camp Edwards. She is doing what she does best: providing hospitality to those far from home, separated from their families, helping them to learn to get along in a culture strange to them. In many ways, it's exactly what she did at Faith and Friendship Houses, and she sees this as a continuation of her ministry

195

of hospitality, caring and compassion.

Mona Jerome

Saving Wild Mustangs to teach Children Responsibility

She's the foster mom of seven wild mustangs and one little burro named Burrito. Mona Jerome sees wild horses roaming free on the open grasslands of America as part of our legacy to the next generation. She also knows that the vision is jeopardized by the threat of extinction posed by the slaughter of these animals by landowners and ranchers who fear an overgrazing problem. (There are about 40,000 of these horses in eleven western states.)

She is so moved by this loss that she has become a strong voice in the preservation of this American resource, and serves as a member of the board of an organization known as Mustangs and Burros Organized Assistance. She is a leading proponent for the adoption of these wild animals.

Mona, a licensed practical nurse and the mother of four children, used to ride horses as a teenager and young woman, but gave it up in order to raise a family and contribute to the medical field in her role as a health care provider. Now that her children have grown and she has become committed to the plight of the wild mustang, Mona has returned to her lifelong interest in horses.

"This developed without any plan in the beginning," she says. Initially, she just wanted to own, ride and love a mustang. The Jeromes purchased land in Biddeford, Maine, and built a barn and started Bush

197

Brook Stables, boarding horses and then eventually providing riding lessons, summer camps and trail rides. They added a second barn and an indoor riding ring. It wasn't long before Mona's heart went out to the other mustangs who needed homes, and she dedicated herself to being a link between these wild horses and good families who can provide a loving home

The government, in an effort to save the mustang, passed protective legislation in the 1950s and set up regional adoptive sites. But, too frequently, adoptive families couldn't cope with these horses. "A lot of people fall in love with these animals because they are young, and they're cute and they are very frightened. They adopt them, not knowing what a commitment they really need to make. So what we do is try to help them with the training process if they need help, or in some cases, they turn the animals over to us after two or three years when they just weren't able to handle them. What we don't want to happen is to have a wild horse adopted by a family who cannot care for them and they end up being slaughtered anyway."

Some families are ideal, and most mustangs can become excellent saddle horses. They are small and sturdy, and contrary to the popular perception, very docile. They are easily trained if given enough time to get used to the domestic life, rather than roaming the range. The term wild mustang conjures up the image of a rearing animal with hooves flailing and nostrils flaring. But that is not the case after they've been gentled and have learned how to be around people.

The mare that she originally adopted, Owyee Lady, is a friendly and intelligent horse which Mona takes on extended trail rides and enters in competitive events. Often when a new mustang arrives, it is very skittish when people approach. Mona explains, "You have to remember that these horses have just been rounded up, sometimes herded by helicopters or other land-based vehicles. They are loaded up and shipped thousands of miles. Their first exposure to human beings can sometimes be inhumane, even though it is not intended to be so. They are frightened, not wild and unmanageable."

With patience and time, these animals can be trained and used as family pets, in stables as school horses and even shown in dressage and other types of performance events at horse shows. Sometimes a new mustang will stand outside in the snow or rain, despite the availability of a shelter, because it is so used to being in the wild. If the mustang comes from the Bureau of Land Management, there is no trust in humans at all. It could take as much as several weeks for the horse to even accept the presence of a human being near them. Mona or one of her staff sometimes just sits inside the stall, quietly reading a book for a little time each day, letting the horse get used to their presence. Mona often leaves treats just inside the stall, but at first, the horse won't touch them. Eventually, the patience and non-invasive overtures win the horse over. Then the staff can work with it free within a round pen, and then on a long rope (called a lunge line) with the trainer far away from the horse on the other end of the rope. The next steps are to learn to walk and trot and halt on command. Then it's back to the lunge line with the weight of a saddle on the back. Next Mona will just put her hand in a stirrup and press down, showing the horse what that feels like. Then she will briefly lay across the saddle, so she can land on her own feet if it doesn't like that idea! She does this from both sides because a horse sees differently from each eye and she wants it to recognize her no matter which side she's on.

After that, Mona ponies the horse by putting all the tack on it (bridle, saddle, etc.) and has it walk beside a seasoned horse which she is riding. This gets the new horse used to seeing her higher than he (or she) is. Depending on the new horse's responses to all these steps, at that point, she might try to get on him. All of this patient training could take a few days, or many weeks. It just depends on the horse's temperament. "Sometimes," Mona laughs, "the horse will look around at me as if to say, *Come on, Mona, when are you going to ride me?* Timing is just something you know by instinct after being around the horse for a while."

Mona never knows when she's going to receive a call from a family who can no longer care for their adopted mustang, so the population at Bush Brook Stables fluctuates. "They're always coming and going," she laughs. It's clear to see how much these animals mean to her. The stables are also home to two flop-eared rabbits and a black cat. "They provide companionship for the horses," she explains, "like neighbors running in and out to say hello and spend time together." Once a mustang is adopted, she stays in touch with the adoptive family and often receives cards and photos of the children riding their new family pet. The success stories help keep Mona on track and upbeat. She needs to be sure the horses are cared for appropriately and not brought into captivity only to end up in a neglectful or abusive situation.

Mona herself has traveled west to see her beloved mustangs in the wild. Her first trip was to Nevada, which has the largest population of wild horses. "I met with a representative of the Wild Horse and Burro organization who took me up into the mountains," she remembers. "The mustangs aren't just standing there, waiting for you to discover them, so we rode most of the day to get to their natural home. It was exciting to see them in their own setting, the way nature intended it to be."

Mona has a collection of books, including an adoption manual that describes the breed and the history of the wild mustang. There is one particular kind of mustang known as the medicine hat mustang. It has an unusual coloration, with a black chest and spotted body. The Cheyenne Indians used to honor these horses as having protective powers, saving them from death in battle. Whether that is true or not, it's impossible to think of mustangs in a detached way after meeting Mona and her mustangs.

Rescuing mustangs is just part of Mona's life. Special needs kids have been helped by learning to ride, too. One child who is deaf has greatly improved her sense of balance by learning to ride. What's especially rewarding to Mona is to see children learn that helping others is a great lifestyle to adopt. One way she gets this message across is to help her students sponsor a trail-riding competition to raise money for the Biddeford Free Clinic. This is a medical treatment facility for those without health insurance, and Mona uses her nursing skills to help out there on a regular basis, as well as being on call at the local hospital. Mona's students have trail rides periodically to raise money for this clinic. Her pride is evident as she talks about what the Bush Brook riders have accomplished.

"I believe children need to learn social responsibility. The children and I discuss what the needs are in the area and then they decide which charities to raise money for. We had an Animal Awareness Month when all the students brought in dog food, cat food, kitty litter, and other donations for the local animal shelter. We also donated to St. Jude's Hospital, which specializes in the treatment of critically ill children. It's great to see the children gaining self esteem and make a commitment to public service and the welfare of others. The fund-raisers are their ideas, and they carry them out. Their devotion to the mustangs is also very special to see. It's gratifying to me to watch these youngsters come to our summer camp and gain self-confidence as they learn to handle the horses. It isn't long before they can manage these large animals as if they were Chihuahuas!"

If there is one message Mona wants to get across loud and clear to kids and adults alike, it's this: "Nothing is impossible. It may be hard, but you can do it!"

Nancy Zienkiewicz

Teaching 15,000 Girl Scouts to Believe in Themselves

> On my honor I will try to serve God and my country, to help people at all times, and to live by the Girl Scout Law.

No matter when you learned it, the meaning is the same. Once you've been a Girl Scout, you just don't forget that promise! Nancy Zienkiewicz (pronounced ZIN-keh-wits) started as a Brownie in 2nd grade. Her mother, who had also been a Girl Scout as a child, was Nancy's troop leader. "I have wonderful memories of being a Girl Scout. Looking back, I really appreciate my troop leaders, the assistant leaders, the people within the community that made sure Girl Scouting happened. Now I know that what I thought was a two-hour meeting so we could learn and have fun, represented hours and hours of preparation time and tons of energy from the volunteer leaders."

Nancy is the quintessential Girl Scout. She has served as a leader for a Cadette/Senior troop, as well as leader for a Brownie troop. She has also been a Kennebec Council Trainer, working with the adult volunteers and teaching them how to be effective troop leaders. In addition, she has directed Troop Camp Training Weekends and organized what is called Treasure Chest, a training day for adult volunteers and older Girl Scouts, grades 7 through 12. She has also served as Day Camp Director.

"Girl Scouting was nearly a full-time job for me," says Nancy with an irresistible grin. "I was volunteering about 40 hours every week. I have two daughters, Jennifer who is 18 and Kimberly who is 15, and I was the leader in both their troops."

In 1994, Nancy's dedication to Girl Scouting took a turn. They hired her! Now she is Program Manager, supervising all summer camp programs in the southern part of Kennebec Council. She also coordinates council activities for all older girls and their leaders. "It's an exciting new opportunity for me. I enjoy my career so much. I've learned new skills and things about Girl Scouting I didn't know before. I feel very lucky. I've seen the wonderful growth it has produced in the lives of so many girls. The focus is the girl. Girls need that chance to excel. Girl Scouting gives it to them. As an organization, we try very hard to stay in tune with changing times, to keep the program relevant to today's girls and what they're facing. It's now possible for girls to register independently without being part of a troop and work on recognitions or community service projects and be involved in the events. This works well for the older girls whose school schedules may be a problem when it comes to attending regular weekly meetings in a troop setting."

Reaching out to help other people is Nancy's way of life. She learned it from her mother who taught her that we need to give back, not just take from life. Nancy's husband, Michael, who had been the Port Operations Officer at Portsmouth Naval Shipyard in Kittery, retired in October of 1995. Since he was still too young for the rocking chair, he found a new job: he is the Camp Ranger for Girl Scout Camp Pondicherry in South Bridgton, Maine. The family moved there in March of 1996. For the Zienkiewicz family, Girl Scouting is definitely a way of life.

"When you're a military family, it's especially important to volunteer and get involved in the community because that's your extended family. Girl Scouting gave me the chance to be part of a community that had members wherever we went. It provided instant friends for all of us."

There are 17,500 girls involved in the Girl Scouts in Maine, with over 5,500 volunteers working with them. There are very few paid positions within the organization which is 85 years old. Because of one woman's vision, Founder Juliette Low, there are now Girl Scouts or Girl

Guides in over 100 countries of the world. The purpose has been the same since the beginning: to assist girls in becoming caring, confident and competent adults.

There are many ways to work within the Girl Scout organization and you don't have to be a kid to join. Some work with the girls; some work with the adult volunteers. There are also many non-traditional volunteers: men, women who don't have children, and women who are grandmothers. Volunteers are always needed! Speaking at a workshop for adult volunteers, volunteering in the office, being a trail crew leader, mentoring an older Girl Scout from a position in the business community or being a uniform swap coordinator — almost any special knowledge or skill you could share is probably going to be something the Girl Scouts will appreciate.

Nancy says, "I believe that kids have a wonderful amount to offer, especially the older girls. The abilities are there. It's more of a challenge because they know what they do and don't want, but it's also very rewarding. Given the chance, kids can do almost anything. Kids are a very important part of our society and very important to the future of our country. Being there for them, teaching them the skills they need to become the leaders we'll need tomorrow and watching them grow into self-assured competent and caring women is very rewarding, and I'd recommend Girl Scouting to anyone."

Of course, volunteering carries its own rewards. Nancy credits her growth in management skills to the training she has received as an adult volunteer with the Girl Scouts. Now that she works with adult training herself, she's seen a lot of growth in self-esteem within the volunteers. There's a network of people ready to support and back up the volunteers. Personal growth is a benefit of volunteering, along with the feeling that you're contributing to society and doing something for America. Nancy says, "To me, the biggest part is the self-esteem issue. If kids feel wonderful about themselves, then they become wonderful people."

Girl Scouting is open to everyone. "We have a lot of fathers who register in order to spend time with their daughters," Nancy says. "Girls need positive male role models, too. It's important for them to see that dads can be caring and involved in their lives. It's a very healthy situation.

My husband, Michael, has been a registered adult Girl Scout for 12 years. So this new position as Camp Ranger is perfect for him."

The fact that Nancy's husband can share his knowledge of the outdoors with the adult volunteers so they, in turn, can pass it on to the girls is indicative of the entire Girl Scout program which is based on five Worlds of Interest: The World of Well-Being (health, fitness, sports, nutrition, first aid); The World of People (learning about people, different countries, exploring your community and how people relate to each other); The World of Today and Tomorrow (math, science and technology); The World of the Arts (music, theater, art); and The World of the Out-of-Doors (nature, camping, environment).

"I tend to be enthusiastic," Nancy smiles, "but I think that's part of life. No matter what happens, you have to go on. Life is what you make of it. And by making it positive, it becomes positive. We've just always lived like that. It's very important that you look for the good things that are there in every situation, and that you believe in them."

Sharon Tennison

Teaching Russians How To Do Business, American Style

Sharon Tennison's $7 million per year nonprofit organization, Center for Citizen Initiatives (CCI), is located in San Francisco, but its sole focus is the former Soviet Union. Not only has CCI mushroomed after the Cold War, but its Russian participants have also built successful businesses far beyond anyone's expectations. Founded in the 80s, CCI's mission was to create links between citizens of both countries, in order to counteract the threat of nuclear war.

In the early 80s, the threat of nuclear war grew daily at an alarming rate. "For some unknown reason, threat of global annihilation became a very personal issue for me," Sharon remembers. "I knew it was insane to build three nuclear weapons a day and generate hostile rhetoric with the second most powerful nation in the world, the Soviet Union. At that time, The United States had 30,000 nuclear weapons; the Soviets had 20,000. I understood that if it came to nuclear war, the citizens of both countries would be incinerated.

Sharon had been a traditional mother and corporate wife for twenty years. Greatly challenged by Mother Teresa's work, she yearned for work that was deeply meaningful. She went back to school and became an intensive care nurse. With the new career developing, strain was put on Sharon's marriage. In 1979, she divorced and began building an

207

independent life just at the time when her four children were either in college or soon headed there.

"I was propelled into actions which previously I would have never considered, for instance, challenging my government's position on the nuclear issue. The role I took on was considered subversive, unpatriotic, and irrational by much of America, including my own father. But the larger issue had to be voiced, and if there were no one else, then it had to be me. Just as in the fable of The Emperor's New Clothes, we were all watching the parade, but someone, somewhere had to stand up and challenge mass consciousness!"

Working in Intensive Care, Sharon took care of trauma and burn victims. The results from nuclear war would be far worse, and on a much larger scale. Sharon and her coworkers often discussed nuclear war issues. When several local doctors formed Physicians for Social Responsibility to take a stand against America's nuclear policy, they asked Sharon to join and help educate the public on the medical consequences of nuclear war. She began speaking to citizen groups in the South Bay Area of San Francisco.

"I learned how ingrained the prejudices were toward the Soviet people," she explains. "There was a blanket damnation prevalent in those first meetings. American citizens were totally ignorant about the 250 million Soviet people! At the end of 1982, I decided I had to go see the enemy for myself."

Sharon had been sharing her ideas with a number of friends, and a number of them wanted to go to the USSR with her. In 1983 she made an appointment at San Francisco's Soviet Consulate to speak with the Soviet Vice Consul. She told him of her group's interest in taking to the streets of the USSR to try to meet ordinary Soviet citizens. He did not see the group as a threat and cleared the way.

"Our main goal was to get into the country and try to develop communications with the people, on a grassroots level, free from entangling governmental bureaucracies and red tape," Sharon explains. "This we did from day one of landing in Moscow. We walked out the doors of the Cosmos Hotel and began exploring, first near the hotel, then on Moscow metros throughout the city. In every direction, we met Soviets on the street who struggled to communicate with us in broken English.

"We took over a thousand slides in market places, at schools, playgrounds, parks and in tiny Soviet apartments. We showed up at the Moscow Baptist Church unannounced, and were invited to speak! Then we followed a wedding party to a local hall, and were invited to dance and celebrate with them. We discovered that these people definitely were not the enemy! They were open-hearted, warm, friendly people who loved family, the classics, poetry, and good literature. They were just ordinary people like us, but citizens of a country caught behind the Iron Curtain.

"We got the sense that the USSR was headed for huge changes. Citizens in four different republics we visited were pressing against the system. We considered ourselves citizen diplomats and began developing our Soviet grassroots networks. As I look back," Sharon muses, "we were both spearheaders and beneficiaries of that particular historical moment. The world did not know it, but the USSR was on a collision course with reality. We were allowed to penetrate every level of ordinary Soviet life."

On that first flight home, the members of Sharon's group vowed to give six months to educating the public about what they had learned. They hit the U.S. running, writing articles for newspapers, and soliciting speaking engagements wherever they could find them.

"I put my manufacturing business in storage and took off across the United States, believing that someone had to shout the truth before it was too late. I traveled 10,000 miles in my tiny Subaru, telling Americans at every stop about the ordinary people of the Soviet Union. There was no funding for our work, so I stayed in strangers' homes every night and didn't worry about where the next meal was coming from. My slide presentations ended with an offer become a citizen diplomat and an invitation for contributions. The donations were always enough to cover expenses.

A new, invisible network began to emerge. Wherever I went, the reactions were the same: I never thought about it before, but what you say makes so much sense! How could the Soviet Union be a nation of barbarians? How can I join a citizen diplomacy trip? One of the people I stayed with was my close friend, Vivian Castleberry, in Dallas, Texas. Like several others who traveled to the USSR with me, she came home and created her own unique citizen diplomacy work."

Then Studs Terkel, the American historian and author of culture at the grass roots level (Working and The Good War), called Sharon and asked her to come to Chicago to be on his nationally syndicated radio program. When he asked her if she knew who he was, and she answered "No," he roared with laughter and said, "This is even better than I thought!" During the interview Sharon's phone number was given over the air, and instantly her home became the clearing house for inquiries from all over the country.

Not believing this was a completely innocent group of citizens who wanted to promote understanding between the two superpowers, the U.S. Government assigned two F.B.I. agents to Sharon. "They wanted to know every move we made!" remembers Sharon. "I patiently briefed them so they would understand we were not subversive people. For five years, I complied with briefings and reports, and in 1990, they disappeared as quickly as they originally appeared."

Sharon and her friends never intended to go to the Soviet Union more than once. But after getting involved in the intrigue between the two nations, they had to continue. Sharon and other group members organized additional trips. On all trips after the first, group members carried cards with these words in Russian: We are American citizens traveling in your country. We are deeply concerned about the relationship between our two nations. Can we talk with you? Do you know anyone who could interpret for us? The cards worked! Communication was never an insurmountable problem.

All citizen diplomacy travelers had to sign an agreement to do six months of public education upon their return. This was the only way to get the message to grassroots America. Believing that: When the citizens lead, the leaders follow (a quote from Eisenhower); and Never doubt that a small group of people can change the world; indeed it's the only thing that ever has (a quote from Margaret Mead); these citizen diplomats charged forward, assuming they would change American and Soviet mindsets a roomful at a time until the two nations broke their dangerous deadlock.

Since then, many of Sharon's friends returned to the former Soviet Union, and Sharon herself has returned over 60 times. That original handful of American citizens has become a nonprofit organization (Center for Citizen Initiatives) to help Russian citizens to develop democracy and a market economy. CCI's ahead-of-the-wave programs have included everything from helping the Alcoholics Anonymous message permeate eight republics of the former Soviet Union, to sending over 90 tons of vegetable seeds to fledgling private farmers, to building several business management programs for struggling Russian entrepreneurs.

In 1993, ten years after landing in Moscow under the eyes of the FBI, Sharon received a White House appointment to serve on the board of directors that administered the $350,000,000 U.S. fund to help Russia develop its small business. She has initiated two large, multi-year business management training programs for Russians, microincubator training and loans for Russian women entrepreneurs, an equipment leasing program for Russian manufacturers, and a program to help individual Russian farmers which has resulted in implementation of the US Extension Service model in multiple regions throughout Russia. Under Sharon's persuasive fundraising, CCI has raised over $30 million to carry out a multitude of programs. "It seems a short while since we were all pitching in to purchase two rolls of stamps to send out homemade newsletters," she laughs, "but sometimes it also seems like light years ago!"

In 1994, Congressman Dick Gephardt brought a large delegation of Congress members, including Newt Gingrich, to Russia. Sharon was invited by the U.S. Consul General to brief them and then introduce them to the real heroes of Russia, the grassroots manufacturers and company owners who are struggling to create the new Russia. The Congress members were stunned by the plight and the dedication of these entrepreneurs. Since then, CCI has had strong bipartisan support in Congress. The Center presently runs six programs and is gearing up to expand its largest effort ever: Sharon's variation of the Marshall Plan, The Productivity Enhancement Program for Russia, which is possible through the combined efforts of the US Volunteer Specialist and The United States Information Agency.

The program brings delegations of industry-specific production company owners from Russia to spend a month in American companies of similar profile. "If the Russian companies make cheese," Sharon explains, "we take them to Wisconsin. They are totally immersed in cheese-making, American style, from talking to the line workers to meeting with the accountants, learning how we do it in the U.S. Every day the Russians document what they've learned by writing in journals, taking photos and making video tapes to take home. They not only teach their workers how to run small private companies, but are often asked to appear on Russian TV and radio.

"And they're making it work!" Sharon enthuses. "Russians and Ukrainians are well educated, very intelligent people They learn quickly, once they see how it's done. One major problem is that they have not been exposed to product diversification. The Communist system was a cookie cutter system; everyone had the same style of curtains, same sofas, and same clothes as everyone else. Once they see the many styles a company can manufacture and sell, they increase their products and sales. Now they can have a hundred different sofa styles to appeal to different tastes!"

Sharon is quick to add that she has not done this alone. CCI's programs are strictly citizen based and not government-originated. Every Russian pays part of the costs. The unit cost of training one Russian businessperson in America for a month is $5,000 per person, shaving about $10,000 off traditional costs, because all the trainers and home hosts are volunteers. The results have been both exciting and rewarding to both sides. "These are relationships that will last forever," Sharon says. "We've seen some joint ventures between their businesses and ours. Even adoptions and exchange families have taken place. These programs have been catalysts for the very best between our two nations."

In 1997, Sharon was asked by the State Department to make some recommendations about how to create a massive business training program for 35,000 Russian managers in response to a request from President Yeltsin. President Yeltsin's team also sent CCI an invitation to come to Moscow to discuss how this new initiative could best proceed. The Moscow meeting date was 14 years to the day since she first set foot in the USSR. (And, yes, she has also begun writing a book about her experiences.)

"In the past fourteen years," Sharon says, "I've learned that the most powerful things in the world are invisible ideas. Learning to work with invisible forces is the beginning of creativity. We have no idea how much difference we can make with an idea. I am an ordinary woman,

212

mother and grandmother with a growing suitcase of ideas! We all must act on these nebulous, but powerful, ideas about how our world could and should work better. We can't afford to leave it up to people in positions of power.

"It's necessary for women to go beyond their own families and see the world as our larger family. We're all called to move into larger service, for we have gone beyond the time to take care of just our own nests. If I could, I would tell American women just one thing: It's time to get off our seats and onto our feet. It will take all of us working hard to create a viable 21st century. Whether it's going to Russia or helping the elderly man next door, we all must take responsibility for situations and people who are less capable than we are."

Betty Hanson

Turning Tears into Smiles with Pet Therapy Dogs

You get lost in them. Pandora's wonderful dark eyes. They hold the wisdom of the ages and unconditional compassion and love. Anyone who has loved a Golden Retriever knows the feeling well.

Betty Hanson and her husband, Jim, have had many wonderful dogs over the years, but, unlike most pet owners, they use their dogs to encourage healing, both physical and emotional. The Hansons are the local representatives of Therapy Dogs, Inc.

"Right now," Betty admits with a smile, "I coordinate the visiting schedules of sixteen dogs and their handlers. They regularly pay a call on various local nursing homes and hospitals. It's a lot of responsibility, but it's well worth it. I get back so much more than I give! To see what a Therapy Dog's visit means to older people who think the world has forgotten them is more than ample reward for what I do."

Betty met Jim in high school, but it wasn't until he left the Navy that the romance between them began. (It's very obvious that after 48 years of marriage, the romance is still there!) Betty's mother was a very giving, hard-working person who taught her to give of herself and give back to the community.

The Hansons have always had more than one dog. "One of our

first dogs was a Basset Hound named Rinkls. then the children bought Jim a female Basset we called Missy. Then we got our first Golden, Toby. there was no question about obedience training. We went! I believe every dog should go to obedience training for one reason: socialization. They need to get along with other dogs, and owners need to be able to control their dogs. If a person just wants to visit nursing homes, Therapy Dogs does not require obedience training. But if you want to visit the hospitals, the requirements are a little more stringent, and obedience training is required. It's important for dog and owner to work as a team. Many people who belong to Therapy Dogs, have turned their dogs' obedience routines into tricks performed for the people they visit. Tricks bring laughs, which are very much needed in hospitals and nursing homes."

Because they had such wonderful and well-behaved dogs, Betty and Jim were often asked to put on demonstrations for various groups — nursing homes, obedience sessions, schools. Soon it was every week. Not only did the Hansons enjoy it, but their dogs loved making new friends, too.

One of the goals of Therapy Dogs is to help people heal. The dogs visit people in nursing homes, hospitals, schools, as well as the mentally and physically handicapped. The dogs are both pure and mixed breed, obedience and conformation (show) dogs. The most important quality a therapy dog must have is a stable temperament. If the dog is gentle, loves people, likes to be petted, has a sweet disposition, is well mannered and does not jump up on people, he or she could be a candidate for Therapy Dogs. It is not true that a dog must have a lot of obedience training to be a good Therapy Dog. "Whether the dog is a household pet or a show dog, if the disposition and manners are there, your dog could make a tremendous difference in someone's life," Betty explains. "Think how you would feel if you had to spend a year in the hospital, for example, and not see your beloved pet all that time. That will give you some idea how important this work is."

When the Hansons first began visiting nursing homes with their dogs, they were unaware of Therapy Dogs, Inc., out of Cheyenne, Wyoming. When they did become aware, they wasted no time in registering their pets. Belonging to a recognized organization not only lends credibility to the work these dogs do, but it establishes standards of

216

conduct so everyone knows what to expect. The other important reason for registering a dog is insurance coverage. A dog registered with Therapy Dogs, Inc., carries his or her own liability insurance.

The first step in registering a dog is for the dog to pass an on-site test at a nursing home. Then the dog and handler have to do at least three more evaluation visits. Sometimes a dog will have to pay more visits if the evaluator feels he or she is still not ready to be registered. Hospitals require obedience training. Nursing homes do not.

Betty has many stories of how a dog has made a difference in a patient's life. "One woman who has MS and only weighed 99 pounds herself owned a dog who weighed 130 pounds. She had a burning desire to do pet therapy with her dog. At the first visit, the dog was completely out of control. Obviously, it would not have been a good idea for that dog and handler to visit nursing homes as the situation stood. So the woman took her dog to obedience school. Several times. After the next evaluation, both dog and handler passed. They now visit two facilities regularly. They both worked very hard to qualify, and everyone came out a winner.

"At one hospital ward, everyone wanted to see the dog, except for one young paraplegic patient would almost have a panic attack whenever we came around with our dog, Pandora. At first we'd put Pandora between the two beds, but nearer the other patient and as far away from this patient as we could. Gradually, after about six months of Pandora's visits to the neighboring bedside, the young woman surprised us by saying, 'I want the dog on the bed.' So we put Pandora on the bed! Pandy did her usual magic and by the time that patient was released, they were fast friends. It went from zero to 110%.

"Our first visit at one of the hospitals," Betty remembers, "was on a Sunday afternoon to the physical therapy room for patients in rehabilitation. They brought the patients into one room. One garrulous patient from across the hall called out, 'I want to see the ____ ____ dog!' So we took Mr. Peepers over to see him. After the visit, we overheard the staff say, 'Okay now we have to bathe the patients, disinfect the floors, and change their clothes.' Jim told me, 'It's never going to work.' But they went again, and after the visit, they suggested that the dogs visit pediatrics. The response was not encouraging. Gradually, as the staff watched the dogs with the patients on the rehabilitation floor, they realized that the dogs were doing something for them that the staff were not able to do, and the dogs' visits became a welcome and permanent fixture.

"There was a young boy who could only move one hand, just enough to operate his wheelchair. When he was ready to leave the hospital, they had trouble deciding where he should live next, because he needed so much care. They filmed a video of the boy and Mr. Peepers playing ball. The boy would laboriously roll the ball off his tray and onto the floor. Peepers would pick it up, go around the chair, put his paws up and drop it on the tray for the boy to roll off again. The video helped the caregivers at his new residence plan his ongoing care. And he still sees Mr. Peepers.

"One elderly lady at one of the nursing homes was very lethargic, just sitting day after day. Now she waits for Saturdays, because that's when we take the dogs to visit. She looks out the window so she can see how many dogs are coming and to make sure they come to visit her. Saturday makes her whole week. She has the dogs sit and then she gives them a cookie. It has made a big difference to her.

"There was one young patient who was not progressing as everyone had hoped and had really given up on getting well. After several visits from Mr. Peepers and Pandora, one day the young man asked if he could walk with Mr. Peepers. Jim had the dog on a leash, of course, but he walked behind while the young man walked beside Mr. Peepers down the hall. "That was a real turnaround," Betty recalls. "He decided life was worth living after all, and from that point he began to improve."

One group that is especially glad to see Therapy Dogs is Alzheimer's patients. They look forward to the dogs' coming and, even if they forget their own names, they seem to remember the names of the dogs!

Betty and Jim are constantly touching base with the staff at each facility they visit. They discuss patient needs and progress, and where the staff thinks a furry friend's visit would help the most, always working within the parameters the staff sets for the dogs' visits.

The patients, too, are very grateful and don't hesitate to say so. The Hansons receive many letters after people go home from the hospital, thanking them for bringing the dogs to visit. One woman wrote, "How wonderful it was to feel a nice silky ear!"

What does the future hold for Therapy Dogs? The Hansons foresee continued steady growth. They have visited hospitals, nursing homes, and one home for veterans, and new requests come in weekly. There is always a need for more qualified therapy dogs.

Qualifications encompass age, vaccinations, health examinations, cleanliness and obedience. No fleas and no female dogs in season. Only one dog per handler is allowed, only certain collars are accepted, and the cleanliness and grooming of the handler is a factor as well. All the guidelines make perfect sense.

"Sometimes I come out of the nursing homes with tears in my eyes because of some response I've seen in a patient who was not responding before. And it's because of the dog's visit," Betty says. "It truly gives me a lift, too. Where would we meet such nice people if we didn't do this?"

From Beagles and Collies to Shitzus and Black Labs, Therapy Dogs minister to all races and nationalities, male and female alike, from toddlers on the children's ward to the most elderly patient in a nursing home. Illness and heartache know no age or gender or race boundaries. Nor do Therapy Dogs. Their tricks and antics delight young and old and bring smiles to faces usually filled with depression and loneliness. These four-legged ambassadors of good health do for patients what all medical science cannot: spread love and joy just by being there. And who's to say they're not grinning back at the patients?

It's very obvious that Betty Hanson loves her dogs. And her dogs love her. What's also obvious is that people love Betty Hanson. Her selfless labor of love in coordinating the visiting schedules of 16 dogs and handlers is a challenge she meets with grace and compassion. She never forgets why she is doing this: to bring healing and encouragement to people who have lost the daily contact with a pet that most of us take for granted. Pets are extremely important to a person's sense of well-being. Who can overestimate their importance in the healing process? They bring a touch of love and normalcy to an otherwise abnormal situation. Betty's patience, compassion and perseverance bring smiles in place of tears, and laughter in place of crying. What does she get for her efforts?

How many tail-wags constitute a paycheck?

Cindy Silverman

Providing a Way Out of Welfare for Abused Women and Children

"I was very fortunate," jokes Cindy Silverman, "to grow up in very dysfunctional family. That gave me all the training I needed for this job!" Cindy runs New Beginnings Transitional Home in Glendale, Arizona, and how she arrived at this place in her life is a story guaranteed to inspire anyone.

"My father was very abusive," she explains. "At that time, there were no shelters for abused women and children Both of my parents were uneducated, so they believed girls needed to be educated only enough to run a household and take care of their children. School was never a priority. Both my parents died when I was in high school, and by then, I had bought into their philosophy of being an underachiever.

When Cindy's parents died, she was living in a housing project with her older drug-addicted brother, who was very violent. She was an easy target. After an incredible beating, she ran to a neighbor for help. They asked no questions, and just took her to her aunt. Very angry and hurt, Cindy repressed it all. "I created a fantasy in my mind that I had a wonderful family, parents who loved me very much, but they died before I got out on my own. I even told others this, because it was easier than the truth. Two years later I married a very kind and gentle man. I had told him my fantasy life story, and he believed me. Obviously, I brought many problems to the marriage, believing with all my heart that I was a nobody, and planned to live my life through my husband. I would just be the woman behind the man, just as my mother had been. I was Mr. Wonderful's wife; that was my identity.

"When I was 29, I weighed almost 300 pounds and was terribly insecure and uneducated. I realized I would rather be dead than go on this way, so I went into therapy. My therapist basically reparented me. He told me I was very bright, but an underachiever and challenged me to go back to school. That was a turning point for me.

"Two things happened next: I went to college, and I also lost 140 pounds. I went into a panic, because I had not dealt with my psychological problems. My husband and my children were very supportive, but I'd wake up in the middle of the night and study. I was afraid I'd fail and then everyone would know my father had been right: I was an idiot!. My husband would get up and reassure me I'd do well, make me coffee, and quiz me on the material. My grades were high enough to put me on the Dean's List every semester, but I still couldn't shake the belief that I was stupid, because it was so ingrained in my belief system. After five long years in intense therapy, hard work at school, and many ups and downs, I received my B.S. in Psychology and was graduated with honors. Even when I got my transcript and the lowest grade was B+, I wondered how I had fooled all those teachers!

"While I was working toward my degree and at the same time I was moving upward with my life, my husband was on a downward spiral in his career. We were not the same two people who had married. When he left, we were four months behind on the rent and had no food in the house. I cried every night. I was very afraid of being homeless. I had received an eviction notice and was terrified the sheriff would come and we'd be living on the street. Through it all, I continued to believe if I got an education, I would be fine. If not, I'd never have a better life. I prayed daily, 'God, just please let me graduate, and I'll do something to make a difference.' My children were 8, 6 and 4 years old. I also had three emotionally disturbed foster children living with me, and I was a full-time student living on welfare. For the next two years I took care of the six children, was a full time student (including two days of field work each week), and worked midnight to 8 A.M. on weekends. I clung to my education and eventually received my master's degree in social work in 1989. I believe I used the welfare system the way it was designed to be used: as a temporary assistance to a long range goal. With my education completed, I knew I'd be self-supporting and never need food stamps again.

"I had a desire to start over. I told my kids we were going to start a new life, so I gave up everything and moved to Arizona in 1992. My new job in Arizona was counseling victims of domestic violence. Because of what I had learned about myself in my long course of therapy, I knew the dangers of staying within an abusive situation. I advised my clients to get out of their abusive situations. I told them of the shelters in the area. One of them stopped me cold with, 'But where do you go after that? You're only allowed to stay in a state-funded shelter for 30 days. Then what?'

"Domestic violence is about power and control. If there is no place to go after 30 days, the only choices are going back to the devil you know (the abuser) and the devil you don't know — homelessness. I remembered my promise to God – to make a difference. Finding a solution for these women became my focus. It made sense to me to take up the challenge. All my life had been a training ground — my own abusive childhood, my fight for education, my need for welfare and food stamps – I had been preparing for this very thing."

Cindy vowed to open a home where women and children who were victims of domestic abuse could live without fear of homelessness. The parameters for entry were fair. A woman would have two years to go to school, studying anything she wanted to. Part of her welfare benefits would be paid into a fund to help with the operating expenses at the house, but the costs would be affordable. Cindy would become a fund-raiser to provide whatever else was needed. The women could live there without fear for two years while they pursued education and not have to worry about any bills. Cindy would even supply diapers and the basic necessities. The first service club she approached gave her $1500 – not exactly overwhelming, but enough to get started.

She rented a house with four bedrooms. There were no lamps, no dishes, no furniture – nothing. Cindy supplied these from her own home. When she interviewed her first candidate for housing, she told the woman she could move in September 1st. Then she told her board of directors. They pointed out that no insurance was in place to protect anyone, and she could not open on September 1st. Cindy had to tell the woman she couldn't come and advised her to stay in the state-funded shelter. That wasn't possible because she had already been there 30 days. The woman had no choice but to move in with her mother. Her abuser showed up with a loaded shotgun. He broke through the door, and aimed the gun at her head. Anticipating what might happen, the woman's mother had a loaded gun ready, and she shot and killed the man.

"God works in mysterious ways," Cindy smiles. "When the story hit the newspapers, the donations of furnishings for the home began to pour in. We received everything we needed, except money. We took in four families. Six months later, I realized we showed no stability since it was a rented house and it could be closed at any time. If we were going to do more, we needed to buy a house to prove to contributors that we were serious. A local businessman gave me $5000."

Over the next year and a half, Cindy networked the community to donate labor and materials to repair the run-down house, always explaining to them what she was trying to do for the victims of abuse. The contractors put on a new roof, a new kitchen, and made the house meet the housing needs for its diverse occupants. When the last nail was in place, Cindy had paid $5000 for $50,000 worth of work.

After three months of living communally, the women were starving for privacy. No one wants to live like that for two years, so they were completing their educational goals. "That's when I went back to the same businessman who had given me the $5000," she says. "He was very impressed with what we had done with his donation. I explained the need to him, and told him I had found an apartment complex for sale. He gave me $12,000 for the downpayment. Then we started to show real success. The women had their own apartments instead of living in a group home. That was a tremendous boost to their self-esteem and helped them see that the future could be good for them. Two months later, the businessman who had given her the downpayment came to see how things were going. He was impressed. He told Cindy, "I want you to do this on a bigger scale. It's time for government to step out of the picture and for businesses to take over. We should be the ones helping these women. I will give you $65,000. Go find a bigger apartment complex." Cindy found a building with 22 units and bought it in July of 1997. She has also kept all the other buildings she has bought and is now serving 34 families. Hers is the largest transitional program dedicated to victims of domestic violence in all of Arizona.

The women start in the communal home which houses seven families. They have to have good attendance, no drinking, no drugs and no contact with the abuser on the premises. If they show they're committed to getting their education and getting off the welfare system, they're moved into their own apartment for the duration of the two years.

"You don't need a big government grant to get started," says Cindy. "You can do it because you want to. But you have to have a passion for what you're trying to do. When someone comes to me for housing, I look for a commitment to her own education. She has to see this as a way to get off the system.

"Welfare was never intended to last someone's entire life. It was always supposed to be a temporary measure. We've become such a dependent society. It's sad that it took 60 years for us to wake up and realize we need to fix the welfare system. Being on welfare is a self-perpetuating situation. Without the drive to make a better life for yourself, it's very difficult to break the cycle. Part of the dilemma is that the fair market value of regular apartments is higher than the welfare benefits received. A woman on welfare has to have a lot of determination. Life is not meant to be just survival. If you work 40 hours a week, you should be able to afford an apartment. We have a lack of affordable housing in this country."

Just how bad is the domestic abuse problem in America? It is present in one in three marriages. It's the number one reason for hospital emergency room treatment nationwide. The cost to employers for absenteeism due to domestic violence is between 3 to 5 billion dollars each year. It raises the cost of health care, requires additional security, and means high turnover and low productivity. Teachers in American classrooms spend 25 to 30% of their classroom time attending to disruptive and angry outbursts from students who live in abusive homes. Clearly, it is a problem that one person alone cannot fix. But one person can make a huge difference, as Cindy Silverman has.

Cindy was awarded the J.C. Penney Golden Rule Award for her vision and commitment. In April of 1997, she received a phone call from the Points of Light Foundation. Cindy had been chosen from 3600 nominees as one of 16 recipients of the President's Point of Light Service Award. "That was a thrill," smiles Cindy. "The purpose of the award is to recognize volunteers who are making a difference. The award was presented at a summit in Philadelphia. Colin Powell was the Chairman and Oprah Winfrey was the emcee. All of the past presidents and first ladies were present along with a host of celebrities. It was a wonderful experience, but it just made me want to do more to help others. What excited me the most was not receiving the award. It was hearing about what the other recipients were doing in their communities."

It takes great strength of character to do what Cindy has done. Breaking the downward spiral is not easy she says. "If I could talk to women in this situation, I'd say, 'You have to get an education, because you can't get a good job without it. If you don't get your education, you're not going to be able to make a living to support yourself and your children.' I'm very pleased with how my life has changed. I've discovered my very best qualities. I've discovered I can be selfless. I have acknowledged my drive and passion and aggressiveness. These are assets. It's taken twelve years, but now I like who I am, and I love helping women who are where I have been. I feel very good about that."

Frieda Jaffe

Waging War Against Intolerance and Bigotry

In 1939, Frieda Jaffe was two years old and lived with her parents in Poland, just south of Warsaw. With the Nazi invasion, life as Frieda knew it ended. "All Jewish people were put into ghettos," she explains. "There were two major factories in my home town, and the Nazis pulled their labor force from these ghettos, using the people for slave labor until they were of no more use. During one particular week in 1942, most of my family was taken by mass transport to the extermination camps, along with Jews from Poland's major cities. My family was annihilated, except for one uncle and one aunt. Most women, children, the old and the infirm were the first to be sent to the gas chambers. It was a miracle that I survived."

Now a realtor in Florida, Frieda has spoken and written about the Holocaust for years. As she recites the horrors of her so-called childhood, it is not possible to concentrate on what she is saying. The images conjured up by her factual account of what happened to her family, friends and neighbors, numb the listener's mind, making it an impossibility to comprehend such terror and stark tragedy.

"It's impossible for me to separate the before and after," she explains. "It was the watershed experience of my life. At age 4, I had been

227

forced by the Nazis to watch my father hanged. As one family member after another disappeared from the ghetto, I was passed on from one relative to another until the end of 1944. At that point, the Nazis were losing the war and the Jews were being moved from ghettos to the concentration camps. That was the nice name for them; they were really death camps. I was sent to two successive extermination camps, and ended up in Bergen-Belsen.

"My private war against intolerance began with the liberation by British troops on April 15, 1945. I was eight years old and I had not known any other life than death, disease and destruction. To me, any uniform meant death. So when a British officer approached me, I hid myself in a mud hole. When he told me I was free, I had no idea what that was. I did not know the word free. I asked him what that meant. He said it meant the war was over. I asked him, 'What war?' My entire life had been unspeakable horror. I didn't know any other kind existed. I was too young to even know what was going on. Those British liberation troops had no idea what they had stumbled upon. We were all extremely diseased. A typhus epidemic was running rampant, and we all were suffering from extreme starvation. The first thing the British did was to set up a field hospital.

"There was a handful of us children who had survived. We were scheduled to be sent to Sweden for adoption. I was extremely willful and just plain refused to go. I burst out, 'My uncle is coming for me!' The officer just looked at me and asked, 'What uncle?' I had remembered my mother's brother, one of the last of my family to be sent to Buchenwald. I had convinced myself that he was coming for me, because anything else was unacceptable. I didn't know if he were dead or alive, but I really believed that he was coming back and I would be living with him. I told this to everyone in the displaced persons camp (DP camp). They humored me, but told me to be ready for the bus to Sweden. I had managed to hide, so they had to keep the bus waiting for three hours while they searched for me. When they couldn't wait any longer, they left without me.

"The next day I was outside a small house, wheeling a baby, when I saw a man walking toward me. He looked familiar so I walked up to him and asked if he were from Poland. He walked away from me. Of course, I looked very different. I had been cleaned up, but nothing could be done about my shaven head where the hair was just beginning to grow back. And it had been years since I had seen my family. Something about his walk struck a chord in my memory and I ran after him. It was my uncle. He had been liberated from Buchenwald a bit earlier, and had gone back to Poland to see if anyone from the family was still alive. My aunt also survived and they had found each other at one of the refugee registration centers. Within a matter of a few weeks after the liberation, a list of survivors was circulated. Because it was common for children in the ghettos to take the last name of whoever they were living with, my aunt and uncle didn't even know how to look for me on the survivor list. They realized I might not be listed under my own name, so my uncle came to Bergen-Belsen to look for me. Somehow, I had known I should not get on that bus to Sweden!"

Even though Frieda was reunited with her aunt and uncle, they were not able to get their property back in Poland, and the three of them had no place to go. Many people wanted to go the United States after the war, but the quota system made it difficult. Only so many from each country could go. The Polish quota was extremely small, and they had no one to underwrite their passage to America. They tried to find work in Paris, but there was no way to have any semblance of normalcy. Soon they moved to Brussels, Belgium, to find work. It was there that Frieda entered a schoolroom for the first time in her life. She was nine years old.

"While we were in Brussels, my aunt remembered that her aunt had gone to America in 1913. All she remembered was her aunt's name and that she was in Texas. If there had been zip codes, we would never have found her! Somehow the letter reached her in Ft. Worth, and the family agreed to sponsor us into America. It took us five years to get there because of the quota system. Everything we did for those 5 years was temporary; everything was geared to going to America. I was nearly 14 by the time I arrived in Ft. Worth. I had already lived several lifetimes by then, and I had my own ideas about my future. A college education was one of them."

During college, Frieda excelled at not thinking or talking about what had happened to her. She didn't think anyone cared, and she didn't want to remember. "The last thing I wanted was pity," she explains. "I was determined to be more American than any of the American kids I knew. I was going to excel at everything! I met my future husband when I was in college and we married in 1959. For thirty nine years Harold has been a strong support for me and has really been instrumental in my opening up and being able to speak about my past before groups. It is never easy. I am willing to relive the horrors I suffered so that others will understand the need to wage war against discrimination of any kind. This is my mission. This is why I work with an organization that sponsors trips for groups of teenagers — both Jews and non-Jews – to Buchenwald and Auschwitz to see for themselves what can happen when intolerance is left unchecked. A survivor of the Holocaust has a different mentality. You never let your passport lapse. Never. You're always ready because you have no idea when you might have to leave at a moment's notice. Even now. You have a tendency to never want to get attached to people or places. When you've been herded into cattle trains and you have absolutely no control of anything, you always think you might have to grab that little bundle of belongings and take off. That never goes away."

Frieda Jaffe has pledged herself and all her energies to Jewish survival, ensuring that those who were so inhumanly slaughtered shall never be forgotten. She continues to combat the ongoing shame of bigotry and intolerance in every way she can. Frieda serves willingly on many committees and boards. She is always on call when her rabbi needs someone to get through to a rebellious teenager. She gives tirelessly of her finances, her talents, and herself so that others will never have to suffer their own holocaust. "Jewish survival is a mandate for me," she affirms. "Everyone thinks the Holocaust was then. That's not true. Whether it's in Bosnia, Africa, or China, intolerance and bigotry are alive and well. We haven't learned a thing. When I speak to children and teenagers, I tell them, 'You think that was then and this is now. Not true.

"You have to accept other people...you don't have to love them...but you do have to accept them. Everyone has to have a place in this world. You have no right to make anyone feel inferior or to ostracize a person.' People think, 'It's not in my backyard.' Oh yes it is! It's everyone's business. It's a tough job. Bigotry has to be eliminated, even if our hearts and souls get tied up in knots! Why don't we understand or try to teach the children that we have to live in this world together? When black churches are burned, or synagogues are bombed, we know we haven't made much progress against intolerance and bigotry. I see starving children in Africa on the news and I think, 'I looked like that once.' And I know I have to keep at it, fulfilling my mandate to warn people.

"Bigotry isn't going to go away. Regardless of their cultural background, women have to teach themselves and their daughters to be independent, self-sufficient and to take responsibility. Above all, women must educate themselves to the best of their ability. They have to learn to take charge and not let others make their decisions for them. The one thing I try to teach people is to not be afraid. Taking responsibility gives you freedom. But freedom is not cheap. You do have to pay the price."

Frieda Jaffe continues to pay the price for her freedom. She spends countless hours working with resettlement and rehabilitating refugees. She is a prolific writer and a spellbinding speaker. "I was terribly bitter for a very long time," she remembers. "As I matured, I differentiated dogma and religion from my belief and my thrust in ensuring that Israel and the Jewish people survive. Because if one race or religion is annihilated, who shall be next? If I continue to work to make sure Judaism survives, all the other religions and peoples in the world will have the same privilege. I'm fighting the war against intolerance for all of us. Let's hope and pray that we succeed."

End Notes

I know they're out there — the women I haven't heard about yet. If you know someone who should have been included in this book, please write and tell me why you think she is a candidate for a second volume! Here are the guidelines I use when someone is referred:

- Does she have a positive attitude toward life, recognizing the problems but not dwelling on them, but rather constantly looking for the solutions?
- Does she have a constructive discontent with the status quo, using her imagination to make things better?
- Is she an incurable optimist, expecting success in spite of obstacles thrown in her way?
- Is she willing to work at things longer and without immediate reward, concentrating on the desired result instead of the obstacles? If she fails, does she try again?
- Does she have a caring compassion for others who are struggling? Can she turn her own disappointments and hurts into encouragement for others?
- Is she constantly learning and using her knowledge to encourage and challenge others to fulfill their potential?
- Does she have a healthy self-esteem as well as a sense of true humility, recognizing that she has not accomplished her goals by her own strength alone?

There are 38 women whose stories have been told in this volume. Two thousand years ago, a Jewish man from Nazareth turned the world upside down with 12 men. Just imagine what He could do with 100 women!

For those of you who want to contact organizations that have been mentioned in this book, we have included the following information, arranged alphabetically.

A.D. Players
2710 W. Alabama,
Houston TX 77098
(713) 526-2721

Audubon Society, Maine
118 U.S. Route One
Falmouth ME 04105-6009
(Mail: P.O. Box 6009)
(207) 781-2330

Audubon Society, National
1-800-274-4201

Anita N. Martinez Ballet Folklorico, Inc.
4422 Live Oak Street
Dallas, Texas 75204-6719
Phone: (214) 828-0181
Fax: (214) 828-0101

Bringing Back the Bluebirds
The North American Bluebird Society sponsors research and provides nest-box plans to the public. For a brochure, send a small donation to defray printing costs and a self-addressed, stamped envelope to NABS, Box 6295, Silver Spring, MD 20906-6295.

Camp Sunshine
PO Box 829
South Casco, ME 04077
Phone: (207)-655-3800
Fax: (207)-655-3825
Internet: http://www.campsunshine.org

Castleberry, Vivian Anderson,
For a copy of her book, <u>Daughters of Dallas</u>, contact Odenwald Press, Dallas, Texas 75260, 1994.

Center for Citizen Initiatives
3268 Sacramento Street
San Francisco, CA 94115
Phone: (415) 346-1875
Fax: (415) 346-3731
Internet:http:// www.igc.org/cci.

Discovery Weekend
Maine Cancer Research & Education Foundation
PO Box 553
Portland, Maine 04112-0553
(207) 773-2533

Gilbert Vigue, Ivy
For a copy of her book, <u>Women's Financial Wisdom: How to Become A Woman of Wealth</u>, write to: 222 Kennedy Memorial Drive, Waterville, Maine 04901 ($12.95). E-mail: firm@mint.net.

Institute for Pregnancy Loss,
111 Bow St., Portsmouth NH 03801 Phone: (603) 427-6821

Make-A-Wish Foundation
1-800-722-9474

NAHRA (North American Handicapped Riding Association)
1-800-369-7433

New England Rescue Groups
Affenpinscher (603) 487-2156
Afghan Hound (888) 552-4763
Alaskan Malamute (617) 965-5542
American Pit Bull Terrier (617) 477-9470

Australian Shepherd (860) 873-2403
Basenji (508) 458-8108
Basset Hound (603) 434-0886
Bearded Collie (617) 275-0637
Belgian Sheepdog (603) 881-7668
Bernese Mountain Dog (508) 448-3183
Bichon Frise (860) 763-0547
Border Collie (508) 478-3277 or (508) 363-2978
Border Terrier (508) 372-1775
Boston Terrier (617) 323-7966
Bouvier Des Flandres (508) 358-6657
Bulldog (508) 386-5541 or (508) 842-8848
Bullmastiff (617) 268-0359 or (508) 939-5300
Cairn Terrier (508) 583-0458
Cavalier King Charles Spaniel (617) 784-8038
Chihuahua (413) 648-9276
Chinese Crested (800) 898-5266
Chinese Shar Pei (508) 376-8793 or (860) 747-6397
Chow Chow (508) 688-7288
Collie (508) 456-8473
Curly-coated Retriever (508) 281-3860
Dachshund (617) 581-1854
Dalmatian (508) 562-9019 or (508) 888-2211
Doberman Pinscher (508) 373-8899 or (508) 454-9791
English Cocker Spaniel (508) 897-3883
English Springer Spaniel (617) 237-4751
Flat-coated Retriever (508) 433-2776
Fox Terrier - Smooth or Wire (508) 663-8093
German Shepherd (413) 245-7802
German Short-haired Pointer (617) 698-2542 or (603) 642-5878
German Wirehaired Pointer (508) 249-8360
Golden Retriever (508) 975-4091
Gordon Setter (617) 784-8806
Great Dane (617) 784-9093 or (508) 476-3957
Great Pyrenees (207) 666-8816 or (207) 582-7731
Greyhound (508) 435-5969 or (617) 472-4055 or (617) 729-2577

Irish Setter (413) 367-2182 or (207) 892-3118
Irish Terrier (508) 369-3006
Irish Wolfhound (508) 342-2765
Jack Russell Terrier (860) 526-3918
Keeshond (508) 222-3300
Kerry Blue Terrier (508) 672-6086
Labrador Retriever (508) 356-2982
Maltese (508) 823-2183
Mastiff (508) 830-0673 or (860) 283-6386
Miniature Bull Terrier (603) 887-4117 or (603) 642-5355
Newfoundland (508) 668-0005
Norfolk Terrier (603) 643-5289
Norwegian Elkhound (508) 636-5548
            or (508) 252-3909 or (508) 435-9300
Old English Sheepdog (617) 259-8173 or (603)886-9605
Otter Hound (508) 668-0005
Papillon (508) 597-5382
Poodle (617) 628-1425 or (203) 237-2578
Pug (413) 253-3066
Rhodesian Ridgeback (508) 649-7020
Rottweiler (508) 764-4336
Saint Bernard (508) 852-2483
Samoyed (508) 358-5258
Schnauzer-Miniature (508) 668-2197
Sheltie (508) 363-2978
Siberian Husky (508) 887-7240
Tibetan Terrier (508) 399-7127
Toy Fox Terrier (508) 378-9061
Vizsla (508) 877-5708
Welsh Corgi, Cardigan (508) 285-8589
West Highland White Terrier (508) 943-6254 or (508) 564-4451
Whippet (508) 476-7558
Wirehaired Pointing Griffon (508) 544-8933

Smith, Senator Margaret Chase
Dr. Gregory Gallant, Director
The Margaret Chase Smith Library
Skowhegan, Maine, 04976
(207) 474-7133
(Her book, <u>Declaration of Conscience</u>, is available through her library.)

Stanford, Susan M., Ph.D.
<u>Will I Cry Tomorrow? Healing Post-Abortion Trauma</u>,
Fleming H. Revell Company, Old Tappan, New Jersey, 1986.

The Reading Connection
3240 Wilson Blvd, Suite 230
Arlington VA 22201
(703) 528-8317

Therapy Dogs Inc.
2416 East Fox Farm Road
Cheyenne, WY 82007
(307) 638-3223

YouthBuild
181 Brackett Street
Portland, Maine 04102
(207) 879-8710

<u>Photographic Credits</u>

Photo of (Taken by)
Susan Duchaine, Gloria Dugan, Ivy Gilbert Vigue, Anna Gould, Judith Hannemann, Betty Hanson, Mona Jerome, Thalia Jillson, Caroline Morong, Ann Morrison, Marilyn Paige, Nancy Savage, D.J. Stanhope, Claudette Thing, Linda Woodard, Nancy Zienkiewicz, (Ron Dahle, Biddeford ME)
Rosie Hartzler, Melinda Molin, Alice Anderson (Wayne Casparius,

237

Windham ME)
Colene Daniel (Jay L. Baker, Baltimore MD)
Terry Dannemiller & Autum Aquino (The Scoop, Portland ME)
Ann Fassett (Michael Ayers, Lima OH)
Anna Gould (Kurt Brown, Windham ME)
Frieda Jaffe (Mary Beth Hamberger, Deerfield Beach FL)
Jane Marston & Birgetta (Ralph Copeland, Strong ME)
Anita Martinez (Olan Mills, Dallas TX)
Beth Reese (Richard Greenhouse, Rockville MD)
Cindy Silverman (Jim Langley, Phoenix AZ)
Margaret Chase Smith (Benjamin Magro)
Maribeth Vander Weele (Bruce Hanson, Titonka IA)

APPENDIX

Guide Dog Foundation for the Blind, Inc.®

Fifteen percent of the profit (a combined publisher and author contribution) from the sale of this title will be donated to the Guide Dog Foundation for the Blind, Inc.®. Why do we do that?

At Ladybug Press, we believe that individual commitment to an ideal makes a better person, a better author, so both the company and the authors whose work we offer are happy to include a third party in every book. This third party is an organization which will share in the profits and be included in the book through this informational Appendix. The author selects the charity (not always an easy choice since our authors are involved and committed humans). Alice Hellstrom Anderson has selected the **Guide Dog Foundation for the Blind, Inc.®** to receive donations from her first book.

Guide Dog Foundation for the Blind, Inc.®

The making of a good guide dog begins with a puppy and, logically enough, the Guide Dog Foundation for the Blind® program begins with puppy breeding. Labrador Retrievers and Golden Retrievers are selected for their sound temperament, intelligence, gentleness, and healthy constitution, to participate in the breeding program at their Puppy Nursery in Smithtown, Long Island, New York. From the first, Guide Dog Foundation puppies are given the best in medical care and a strong dose of human affection.

At about 7 weeks, the Guide Dog Foundation puppy is graduated to the "Puppy Walker" program and placed with a volunteer foster family. The Puppy Walker family, aided by the Foundation, shapes the development of the future guide dog over the next year. The puppy is exposed to basic obedience commands, good deportment (staying off of furniture, for instance), and environments it will need to feel comfortable in as an aid and companion to a blind person; regularly going to places such as banks and post offices, train stations and public gatherings. There is a lot for the puppy to learn and a lot for the volunteer family to experience with it. Throughout this process, help and advice is available from Foundation experts.

At fourteen months, the puppy is returned to the Guide Dog Foundation to begin the next phase of its training. Basic obedience is the first priority at this stage. The young dogs are taken through their paces by experienced dog handlers. They learn to walk a straight line, to respond to commands such as "forward" and "halt," and to concentrate on their responsibilities and the commands of their handlers.

Once the young dog has mastered these basics it is introduced to the unique Guide Dog foundation harness and learns to move and react as part of a team of dog and handler. This involves anticipating the spatial needs of being "paired." And, later, the concept of intelligent disobedience that will allow the guide dog to aid its master by refusing to lead into dangerous situations even if commanded "forward." Graduation day comes when the dog is tested with a blindfolded handler at its side.

Meanwhile, the dog owner has been going through an evaluation process of her/his own so that the owner and dog can be well-matched. Once the dog has graduated it is matched with an owner and the training process that will integrate the two as a working pair begins. The final step in the Guide Dog Foundation program is a get-together for puppy walker, dog, and new owner. This is probably the greatest moment of excitement for Guide Dog Foundation for the Blind® volunteers!

The Guide Dog Foundation for the Blind® depends on you for its existence. The volunteer foster families of the Puppy Walker Programs and those who donate funds to the foundation are what make it possible. If you would like to be involved in this worthwhile organization, contact:

Guide Dog Foundation for the Blind®
371 East Jericho Turnpike
Smithtown, New York 11787-2976
(516) 265-2121 or (800) 548-4337 outside New York
fax: (516) 361-5192